Writing About
AMERICAN
LITERATURE

KAREN M. GOCSIK

The University of California, San Diego

COLEMAN HUTCHISON

The University of Texas at Austin

W. W. NORTON & COMPANY

New York • London

W. W. Norton & Company has been independent since its founding in 1923, when William Warder Norton and Mary D. Herter Norton first published lectures delivered at the People's Institute, the adult education division of New York City's Cooper Union. The firm soon expanded its program beyond the Institute, publishing books by celebrated academics from America and abroad. By midcentury, the two major pillars of Norton's publishing program—trade books and college texts—were firmly established. In the 1950s, the Norton family transferred control of the company to its employees, and today—with a staff of four hundred and a comparable number of trade, college, and professional titles published each year—W. W. Norton & Company stands as the largest and oldest publishing house owned wholly by its employees.

Manufacturing by: Courier—Westford, MA
Book design by: Chris Welch
Production manager: Benjamin Reynolds
Composition by: Westchester Publishing Services

Library of Congress Cataloging-in-Publication Data

Gocsik, Karen M.
    Writing about American literature / Karen M. Gocsik, University of California, San Diego ; Coleman Hutchison, The University of Texas at Austin. — First edition.
        pages cm
    Includes bibliographical references and index.
    ISBN 978-0-393-93755-8 (pbk. : alk. paper)   1. English language—Rhetoric—Handbooks, manuals, etc.   2. Criticism—Authorship—Handbooks, manuals, etc.
3. Academic writing—Authorship—Handbooks, manuals, etc.   4. American literature—History and criticism—Theory, etc.—Handbooks, manuals, etc.
I. Hutchison, Coleman, 1977–   II. Title.
    PE1479.C7G567 2014
    808.06'68—dc23
                                                                                                2014007978

W. W. Norton & Company, Inc., 500 Fifth Avenue, New York, N.Y. 10110
wwnorton.com
W. W. Norton & Company Ltd., Castle House, 75/76 Wells Street, London WIT 3QT

1 2 3 4 5 6 7 8 9 0

Contents

Contents

Contents

Contents

Contents

1

Writing About American Literature

This short guide to writing provides information about the nature and process of academic writing in general, as well as information about the specific challenges—and the specific pleasures—involved in writing about American literature.

The Challenges (and Pleasures) of Writing About American Literature

Like the country from which it comes, American literature encompasses a rich and disparate set of people and cultures. The United States is often described as both a melting pot and a nation of immigrants. Not surprisingly, its literature speaks resoundingly to a mixture of identities and ideas.

American literature also extends across a wide swath of time and space. Depending on the course you are taking, it can stretch back to Christopher Columbus's journals or Native American creation myths. Likewise, many American literature courses feature material published in the last decade. The United States has always been distinguished by its vibrant and distinctive regional cultures—some of which extend well beyond national borders. Not surprisingly, then, local and regional texts play a crucial role in American literary history.

The challenge of writing about American literature is also the source of its greatest pleasure: diversity. In an American literature course you might be asked to write on everything from Benjamin Franklin (1706–1790) to Junot Díaz (b. 1968), from poetry and oratory to graphic narrative and popular song. You might find yourself moving from Sarah Orne Jewett's Dunnet Landing, Maine, to Sandra Cisneros's Seguín, Texas, in a very short period of time. Instructors may even ask you to put these diverse writers, genres, and locations in conversation. In what way do Franklin's and Díaz's coming-of-age stories differ? What formal features do Emma Lazarus's poems share with Art Spiegelman's comics? How do Jewett and Cisneros define "home"? As these questions suggest, the scholar of American literature must be nimble, resourceful, and wide-ranging.

This guide will help you to complete whatever writing assignments you receive in your American literature class. It will also help you to meet the challenges of American literature—and to find pleasure in doing so.

But before we go any further, we need to answer a general question: What is academic writing?

What Is Academic Writing?

Put simply, academic writing (sometimes called "scholarship") is writing done by scholars for other scholars—a group that now includes you. Welcome to the scholarly ranks! As a college student, you are doing things that scholars have been doing for centuries: namely, reading, thinking, arguing, and writing about great ideas. Of course, being a scholar requires that you read, think, argue, and write in certain ways. In particular, you will need to make and support your claims according to the customary expectations of the academic community.

So how do you determine what these expectations are? The literary theorist Kenneth Burke famously described scholarship as an ongoing conversation, and this metaphor may prove helpful to you. Imagine you have just arrived at a dinner party. The discussion (which in this case is about American literature) has already been going on for quite a while when you arrive. What do you do? Do you sit down and immediately voice your opinions? Or do you listen to what others are saying, determine what contribution you might make, and only then say your piece?

The etiquette that you would employ at a dinner party is precisely the strategy you should use when writing academic papers. Always listen first to what other scholars are saying, and be sure to pay attention to both *what* is said and *how* it is said. This will help you to gain a better sense of the scholarly conversation and its dynamics.

You might think of a book like *The Norton Anthology of American Literature* as a dinner companion of sorts. Among other things, it can get you up to speed on the conversation about American literature that preceded your arrival. But you should make use of other resources, too. Your instructor, for instance, is a living, breathing expert on what scholars of American literature care about. Books, journals, and credible Internet sites also offer an opportunity to eavesdrop on the ongoing scholarly conversation about American literature. Once you understand the substance of that conversation, you can begin to construct informed arguments of your own.

Getting Started

CONSIDER WHAT YOU KNOW

When you sit down to write an academic paper, you will first want to consider what you know about your topic. Different writing assignments require different degrees of knowledge. For example, a short paper written in response to an episode from Herman Melville's *Moby-Dick* may not require you to be familiar with the history of whaling.

However, if you are asked to write an academic paper on the novel, you will want to know more. You may want to have a sense for the basic outlines of nineteenth-century history and culture, as well as some knowledge of the author's biography. You will certainly want to familiarize yourself with the travel narratives that preceded the novel so that you can understand the themes and conventions that were important to Melville and his contemporaries. Finally, if you are writing a research paper on the novel, you may be asked to account for different critical perspectives on *Moby-Dick* so that you can locate your argument in an ongoing scholarly conversation.

CONSIDER WHAT YOU THINK

The aim in thinking about your topic is to come up with fresh observations. After all, good papers do much more than summarize what is obvious or already known. You must add something of your own—some new insight or novel interpretation—to the conversation.

But let's be clear: your personal reactions, associations, or experiences should not dominate your paper. When you "add something of your own" to a scholarly conversation, that something must be *critical*. Indeed, nearly all forms of academic writing are analytical rather than personal. Put another way, your writing must show that your reactions, associations, and experiences of a work of literature have been framed in a critical, rather than a personal, way.

This is not to say that your personal responses to a work of literature are irrelevant. Indeed, those responses often provide a good starting point for the academic work to come. For instance, being puzzled by the unfamiliar cultural assumptions of Zitkala-Ša can be a first step on the way to a strong analysis. Interrogate your gut reaction. Why are you puzzled by her "Impressions of an Indian Childhood" or her defense of "paganism"? Can you imagine what it would be like to value the things she does? Does your interpretation of the work change as you learn more about the world from which she came?

Interrogating your personal responses is the first step in making sure that your argument will be appropriately academic. To help ensure that your responses are critical rather than personal, subject them to the following critical thinking processes: summary, evaluation, analysis, and synthesis.

SUMMARIZE

The first step in thinking critically about any work of literature is to summarize what it is saying. You can construct several different summaries, depending on your goals, but beware: even the most basic of summaries—for example, the plot summary or paraphrase—is not as simple as it seems. It is particularly difficult to write both economically and descriptively, discerning what is essential to your discussion and what is not.

Whether you are writing about a fourteen-line poem or a several-hundred-page novel, you will want to begin by offering an account of what goes on in the text at hand. While it is often easier to offer such an account for a short story or a novel, poetry, oratory, and other forms of literary art can also be summarized. (Sometimes scholars refer to accounts of shorter texts as *paraphrases*.) You can ask the following sorts of questions of any type of text: What situation is being described here? What concrete action or actions (if any) take place in that situation? Who or what performs these actions?

Although you will rarely be asked to include such a summary in a paper, the exercise of summarizing a literary work is a useful one. It hones your writing skills, alerts you to gaps in your understanding of the work, and helps you see the structure, conflicts, and themes of the work.

But when thinking critically about literature, you needn't limit yourself to plot summary. Depending on the assignment, it may be equally useful to offer summaries of the work's origins and composition, the author's life and times, similarities to other texts, or reception by audiences and critics (e.g., reviews and scholarship).

Again, summarizing helps scholars to clarify what they know about a work of literature. It also lays the foundation for the more complex interpretative and argumentative processes to come.

EVALUATE

Evaluation is an ongoing process. You can evaluate a text the moment you first encounter it, and you can continue to evaluate and reevaluate it as you read. But it is important to understand that evaluating a work of literature is different from merely reacting to it. When you evaluate for an academic purpose, you must find and articulate the reasons for your personal response. What in the text is leading you to respond in a certain way? Are there influences outside of the text that might be conditioning your response?

Reading Kate Chopin's *The Awakening*, for instance, you might find yourself becoming impatient with Edna Pontellier, the novella's protagonist. What is making you feel this way? The words Edna speaks? Her interactions with other characters? The choices she makes or does not make? Something else? Can you point to a moment in the novella when you felt particularly impatient with Edna? How does Chopin's text encourage such impatience? In asking these questions, you are engaged in two intellectual processes at the same time: experiencing your own personal response and analyzing the novella.

Evaluation also encourages you to compare a text with other texts you have read. In an American literature course, this often means comparing disparate works. If you have just read Tennessee Williams's *A Streetcar Named Desire*, you might ask yourself how it is similar to or notably different from Arthur Miller's *Death of a Salesman*. After all, they are both popular American plays from the late 1940s, one set in New Orleans, the other in New York and Boston. A comparison of the two plays likely will reveal both stark differences and striking similarities.

For this reason, comparisons across time periods can be

equally fruitful, especially since most American literature courses cover several decades; some even span several centuries. For example, how does *A Streetcar Named Desire* compare to Susan Glaspell's *Trifles,* which was written three decades earlier? Although these three examples are all plays, you needn't feel bound by genre. For instance, Williams's playwriting is often compared to the poetry of Walt Whitman, who died nearly two decades before Williams was born. Similarly, if you are enrolled in a survey of American literature, then you might compare *A Streetcar Named Desire* to Hannah Webster Foster's eighteenth-century novel *The Coquette.* Among other things, both texts offer complex representations of female sexuality.

As this suggests, the possibilities for comparison are nearly endless. This process of evaluation will help you to discover which aspects of the text are most interesting to you. Remember: it only takes one original idea to start you on your way to a successful paper.

ANALYZE

Analysis is a crucially important stage as you construct an informed argument. Your first task here is to consider the parts of your topic that most interest you, then to examine how these parts relate to one another or to the whole. To analyze Nathaniel Hawthorne's *The Scarlet Letter,* you will want to break the novel down by examining particular scenes, particular characters, and particular actions. In short, you will want to ask: What are the components of this novel? How do these components contribute to the work as a whole? To analyze Toni Morrison's short story "Recitatif," you will go through a similar process of asking questions that break the story down into its various components.

Ask about the story's structure: What is the purpose of the story's two major section breaks? What is a *recitatif*? And how does that word relate to this story?

Ask about the characters and the role(s) they play: What do Twyla and Roberta share in common in this story? How are they different? Who seems more mature or grown-up, and at what point in time?

Ask about themes: What don't we know about our two protagonists by the end of the story? What does that fact tell you about the relationship among race, class, and identity in the story?

Ask about contexts: How does the story reflect the period in which it was written? Is "Recitatif" effective in talking about race and class in the United States during the 1980s? How so?

By asking these questions, you are examining individual components of the story. Your goal is to think about how each of those components functions within the complete work. When you analyze, you break the whole into parts so that you might see the whole differently. When you analyze, you also find something of your own to contribute.

SYNTHESIZE

If analyzing helps you to break a work into its parts, then synthesizing helps you to look for connections between those parts. In analyzing *The Scarlet Letter* you might come up with elements that initially seem disparate or even at odds. Or you might have read various critical perspectives on the novel, some of which disagree vehemently with one another. Now is the time to consider whether these disparate elements or perspectives might be reconciled or synthesized. This intellectual exercise requires that you create an umbrella argument—a larger argument under which several observations and perspectives might stand.

The headnote for Mark Twain in *The Norton Anthology of American Literature* (which you may be reading from in your course) provides an excellent example of synthesis. The author of the headnote elegantly summarizes the critical history of Twain's *Adventures of Huckleberry Finn,* one of American literature's most controversial texts. The headnote is admirably forthcoming about ongoing debates over the novel's representation of race. But the headnote also contextualizes those debates, reminding readers that the novel has always been hotly contested: "In Twain's own day *Huck Finn* was banned in many libraries and schools around the country and denounced in pulpits not for its racial content but for its supposedly encouraging boys to swear, smoke, and run away."

Rather than take a side in debates about the ending of the novel, the headnote deftly refocuses our attention on the novel's popular reception and literary-historical importance:

> Nevertheless, *Huck Finn* has enjoyed extraordinary popularity since its publication. It broke literary ground as a novel written in the vernacular and established the vernacular's capacity to result in high art. Its unpretentious, colloquial, yet poetic style, its wide-ranging humor, its embodiment of the enduring and widely shared dream of innocence and freedom, and its recording of a vanished way of life in the pre-Civil War Mississippi Valley have instructed and moved people of all ages and conditions all over the world.

The headnote's umbrella argument is, then, that *Adventures of Huckleberry Finn* remains a book worthy of reading precisely because it is both controversial and instructive.

Adopting a Rhetorical Stance

When writing an academic paper, you must first ask, For whom am I writing, and for what purpose? You need to consider not only what you want to say but also the audience to whom you are saying it. Thus, you should determine not just what *you* think about a topic but also what your *audience* is likely to think about that topic. What biases does your audience have? What values, expectations, and knowledge do they possess?

When you begin to answer these questions, you have started to reckon with what has been called the "rhetorical stance": the position you take as a writer in relation to the subject and the reader of your paper.

CONSIDER YOUR POSITION

First let's consider your relationship to the topic you are writing about. When you write a paper, you take a stand on a topic. As we noted earlier, a good scholarly argument needs to offer a strong debatable claim. But because few issues can be reduced entirely to pro and con or black and white, you want to take a *nuanced* stance on your topic, one that allows you to remain nimble and spry. Finally, you may want to consider whether or not your position adopts a particular critical perspective (e.g., feminist). All of these considerations enable you to better understand—and thus to better control—your rhetorical stance.

To ensure that your stance is appropriately analytical, you should ask yourself some initial questions. Begin by asking why you have taken this particular position. For instance, why did you find some elements of the work of literature more important than others? Does this prioritizing reflect a bias or preconception on your part? If you dismissed part of the work as boring or unimportant, why did you do so? Do you have personal experiences that might lead you to be impatient with certain elements of the text? Might any part of your response to the literary work cause readers to discount your paper as biased or uncritical? If the answer to this last question is yes, then you might want to reconsider your position. Alternatively, if you feel strongly about the argument you are trying to make, then you will want to carefully plan how you will support that argument with evidence from the text.

CONSIDER YOUR AUDIENCE

Your position on a topic does not, by itself, determine your rhetorical stance. You must also consider your readers. In the college classroom, the audience is usually the instructor or your classmates—although occasionally your instructor will direct you to write for a more particular or more general audience. No matter who your readers are, you will want to consider them carefully before you start to write.

What do you know about your readers and their stance toward your topic? What are they likely to know about the topic? What biases are they likely to have? Moreover, what effect do you hope to have on your readers? Is your aim to be controversial? Provocative? Informative? Entertaining? Will the readers appreciate or resent your intention?

Once you have determined who your readers are, you will

next want to consider how you might best reach them. If, for example, you are an authority on a particular subject and you are writing to readers who know little or nothing about that subject, then you will want to take an informative stance. If, on the other hand, you are not yet confident about the topic and have more questions than answers, then you might want to take an inquisitive stance.

In any case, when you are deciding on a rhetorical stance, choose one that allows you to be sincere. You do not want to take an authoritative stance on a subject if you cannot be confident about what you are saying. At the same time, it is crucially important that you take some sort of stance; readers are often very frustrated by writers who refuse to take a clear stance. What if you are of two minds on a subject? Then declare that to the reader. Make ambivalence your clear rhetorical stance.

Finally, do not write simply to please your instructor. Though some instructors find it flattering to discover that all of their students share their positions on a subject, most of us are hoping that your argument will engage us by telling us something new about your topic—even if that "something new" is simply a fresh take on a minor detail.

Considering Tone and Style

You now have a better understanding of what is required in an academic paper. You need to be analytical. You need to create an informed argument. You need to consider your relationship to both the topic and the reader. But what about finding an appropriate academic tone and style?

The tone and style of academic writing might seem intimidating at first. But they need not be. Instructors want students to write clearly and intelligently on matters that they, the students, care about. What they don't want is imitation scholarship—that is, exalted gibberish that merely sounds intelligent or learned.

Instructors are, after all, human beings—people capable of boredom, laughter, irritation, and awe. Remember that you are writing to a person who will be delighted when you make your point clearly, concisely, and persuasively. Remember, too, that she or he will be less delighted if you have inflated your prose, pumped up your page count, or tried to use advanced terminology that you do not fully understand. (For more on how to craft an appropriate but engaging academic tone and style, see Chapter 7, "Attending to Style.")

2

Kinds of Writing About American Literature

Now that you have a better sense for academic writing, it is time to know more about the study of American literature, which is a diverse and fascinating field. Scholars who work in this discipline write not only about particular works of literature but also about its authors, cultural and historical contexts, and reception. Given this broad sweep, it is important that you know the kinds of writing you will be asked to do in an American literature course.

Textual Analysis of a Work of American Literature

One of the most common approaches to writing about American literature is textual analysis. Textual analysis requires the reader to break down the work into its different parts and to discuss how each part adds up to create the whole. This process is similar to taking apart a tractor in a field: you lay out the parts, try to understand the function and purpose of each part, and then put the parts back together again. After engaging in this process, you will no doubt understand much better how the tractor works, and you will be able to talk about its workings with precision and clarity. When it comes to taking apart a literary text, the particular pieces you are dealing with depend on the text you are analyzing. In a short poem you may need to look at rhythm, rhyme scheme, and the poet's use of figurative language. In novels or short stories you will want to look at the characters, settings, motifs, and conflicts. In plays you will need to look at characters' behavior, stage directions, instances of dramatic irony, and soliloquies or other lengthy speeches.

In all cases, you should think about the themes of the work, as well as the overall effect of reading the text. But be aware: themes are often best understood and written about when you view them through one of the aforementioned textual elements. In other words, as the author of a textual analysis paper, your goal is to choose one of these elements and examine in detail how that element contributes to the major themes or overall effect of the text.

Although some instructors provide detailed instructions in their assignments—which topic to cover, which elements to discuss, and possibly even which part of the work to analyze—others permit students to choose the literary work and the overall topic they wish to discuss. Thus you might write a paper about characterization in William Faulkner's *As I Lay*

Dying or the portrayal of literacy in *Narrative of the Life of Frederick Douglass, an American Slave, Written by Himself.* Each of these topics would find you describing and interpreting the effectiveness of a single element or technique in a single work. Depending on the length of the assignment, you might analyze representative moments in the text, focusing, for instance, on a specific instance of characterization in *As I Lay Dying* or a single scene of literacy in *Narrative of the Life of Frederick Douglass.*

Contextual Analysis of a Work of American Literature

Almost all of literature is socially oriented. That is, most literary works are concerned with people living among other people. To thoroughly understand a literary work, you must therefore consider the work's social, cultural, and political contexts. Understanding the context in which a work of literature is produced and consumed is especially important in an American literature course, which necessarily represents diverse groups of people, cultures, and traditions.

To uncover a work's cultural or political arguments, you will want to undertake a contextual analysis. Contextual analysis involves examining the relationship between a work and its contexts: the social norms and political environment of the culture in which it was written, the historical events that preceded its composition, the author's biography, the literary traditions and popular cultures to which it seems to respond, and so on.

Here are four fruitful questions you can ask yourself as you begin a contextual analysis:

1. How is this text a *product* of its historical or cultural context? In other words, what historical or cultural forces conspired to bring about this particular work of literature? For instance, Hannah Webster Foster's *The Coquette* was one of the first novels published in the United States. Published only a decade after the Constitutional Convention, Foster's fictionalized "History of Eliza Wharton" found an eager audience among both men and women. Contemporary readers seem to have been keenly interested in the novel's representation of a virtuous woman's downfall, in no small part because of increasing anxieties over the role of women in the new nation. How does the novel think about the role of women in the new nation?

2. How does the text *reflect* its cultural context? In other words, in what ways does the text serve as a historical document that allows readers to reconstruct the society in which it was composed? Consider Allen Ginsberg's epic poem "Howl," which opens with the line "I saw the best minds of my generation destroyed by madness, starving hysterical naked." Written in the mid-1950s, the poem is often read as both an indictment of a prosperous, conservative

postwar culture and an announcement of the birth of a counterculture. Where can we see such cultural tensions in the poem?

3. How did the text *influence* future historical events or inspire social change? Harriet Beecher Stowe's *Uncle Tom's Cabin* (1852) is often credited with helping to change people's minds about slavery in the South—and thus with helping to exacerbate sectional tensions—in the decade before the Civil War. The novel is one of the most popular in American literary history; by the beginning of the Civil War it had sold over a million copies in the United States and Great Britain—much to the chagrin of southern writers like William Gilmore Simms, who were mortally offended by Stowe's representation of southern life. We might think of Abraham Lincoln's famous (and no doubt apocryphal) greeting of Stowe during the Civil War, "So this is the little lady who started this great war." What specific parts of the novel might have had such a broad influence on the politics of the 1850s and 1860s?

4. How does the text *comment* upon recent history, and to what purpose? Many of Langston Hughes's poems critique the treatment of African Americans during the early to mid-twentieth century. What, precisely, is Hughes condemning here? What does his vision of racial justice look like? How does he render his critiques in verse?

Once you have determined how a work is speaking to, about, or from its historical and cultural contexts, you will want to consider the work's political views. Granted, not all literature expresses a clear political ideology. Nevertheless, even when a work avoids expressing overtly political or ideological messages, it cannot help but convey subtle attitudes about the social worlds it describes. As you try to sort out a work's political argument, you might consider the following questions:

Does the work of literature seem to espouse a particular set of beliefs and values?

Is the work bringing competing beliefs and values into conversation or conflict with each other? If so, what is the writer telling us, explicitly and implicitly, about these beliefs and values?

Does the work seem explicitly political? Or is it more generally concerned with portraying a social problem?

Does any character in the work consistently embody a particular worldview? If so, what happens to this character? Are we meant to sympathize with him or her?

Does the work seem to be responding to a major cultural crisis—for example, a war, a famine, a political revolution, a grave injustice—**about which the author would have been concerned?**

How was the work first received when it was published?
What does this early reception tell you about the work's relationship to the prevailing values of the culture in which it was produced and consumed?

Comparative Analysis of a Work of American Literature

Sometimes an instructor will ask you to do a formal analysis paper comparing and/or contrasting two or more works of literature. A comparative study requires that you look at specific elements in each text and compare or contrast their qualities. Two strategies tend to lead to success with this type of assignment. First, you might take two texts assumed to be very similar but then show important differences between the two. For example, Joel Chandler Harris's "The Wonderful Tar-Baby Story" and Charles W. Chesnutt's "The Goophered Grapevine" are both dialect tales from the 1880s. Yet there are crucial differences in tone and characterization between the two stories. Second, you might take two texts assumed to be very dissimilar but then show important similarities between them. For example, you might take an influential religious text like Jonathan Edwards's "Sinners in the Hands of an Angry God" and show its similarities to Ginsberg's "Howl"—a poem often described in profane rather than sacred terms.

Whatever strategy you choose, remember: for a compare/contrast paper to be effective, the writer must be sure to limit the comparison to the most salient points. A paper that articulates carefully a few important similarities or differences and then analyzes their significance will fare much better than a paper that simply presents a laundry list of similarities and differences with no analysis or commentary. Less really is more with compare/contrast assignments.

The following hypothetical paper assignments show how the comparative approach is well suited to producing insightful and original papers:

1. Compare John Winthrop's "A Model of Christian Charity" to Martin Luther King Jr.'s "I Have a Dream" with respect to ideas of social responsibility. How does Winthrop's "model" differ from that of King?

2. Compare and contrast the central character in Abraham Cahan's *The Imported Bridegroom* and Sui Sin Far's "Mrs. Spring Fragrance." What do the differences between Asriel Stroon and Mrs. Spring Fragrance tell us about the diverse experiences of immigrants in late nineteenth-/ early twentieth-century America?

3. Compare E. E. Cummings's " 'next to of course god america i" to Emma Lazarus's "The New Colossus" in terms of poetic form. Which conventions of the sonnet does Cummings maintain, and which does he ignore? How does Cummings's use of the sonnet form suit the needs of this

particular text? How is this different from Lazarus's use of the form?

Note that the first assignment asks you to compare two works that were written in radically different cultural milieus, by orators born more than three hundred years apart. The differences between "A Model of Christian Charity" and "I Have a Dream" can be attributed to broader differences between the authors' historical situations and disparate worldviews. The second assignment asks you to compare roughly contemporaneous pieces of literature—Abraham Cahan's novella was published in 1898; Sui Sin Far's story appeared in a 1912 collection—in order to think about how writers from different ethnic backgrounds describe the experience of cultural assimilation. Finally, the third assignment asks you to examine the nature of literary form and the way different authors do very different things with the sonnet.

Writing About Characters

One of the most venerable (read: "old school") of writing assignments is the character analysis. American literature students have been producing character analyses for generations. And although these assignments may seem a bit old-fashioned in the twenty-first century, they get quickly to the heart of literary study: the representation of people and their inner lives. To this end, character analysis has two main functions: to describe personality and to discern motivation.

If you are asked to write a character analysis, choose a character that you find compelling. By "compelling" we do not necessarily mean "likeable" or "admirable." Indeed, some of the most interesting analyses are of repulsive or morally suspect characters, such as Roger Chillingworth in *The Scarlet Letter* or Captain Vere in *Billy Budd, Sailor*. But the character you choose should be someone you find personally troubling, puzzling, charismatic, or important to the text at hand—anything but boring. There is nothing worse than having to write (or read!) an essay on a character that you find boring.

Begin by rereading the text, taking care to note each time your character appears in the narrative. (If you are working with an electronic text, you can, of course, search for the character's name, but rereading the text is always the best approach since characters are often referenced in vague and indirect ways.) As you reread, pay particular attention to the actions the character takes, the things she says, and the ways she thinks. You also want to record any descriptions of your character, either by the narrator or other characters in the text. Ask yourself: How do other characters react to, interact with, or talk about this character? Put simply, what do they seem to think of the character?

Adjectives are a key part of any character study, so you want to choose carefully the words you use to describe your character's personality and behavior. Be as precise as possible when choosing your adjectives—and then quote liberally from the text to show why your adjective is well chosen. You also want to be careful not to diagnose your character. Dubbing a nineteenth-century literary character "bipolar" or "autistic" is anachronistic because both terms originated in the twentieth century. More to the point, such diagnoses belie the fact that you are discussing a fictional character rather than a real person.

As the final chapter of this book suggests, there is a specialized critical vocabulary for character (much of which you probably know already). Scholars use words like *flat*, *round*, *static*, *dynamic*, *minor*, *major*, *antagonist*, *protagonist*, *stereotype*, and *stock* to analyze characters. (More advanced terminology includes *foil*, *antihero*, *tragic hero*, *romantic hero*, and the like.) These words can prove immensely helpful as you write about your character, but they are only one part of your analysis.

Students often struggle to keep their character studies properly analytical. The following questions will ensure that you are analyzing rather than merely describing your character:

- How do we know what we know about this character?
- What do the character's superficial features—for instance, name or physical appearance—reveal?
- What are the character's outstanding psychological or personality traits?
- What motivates the character? Ethics? Love? Hate? Revenge? Ambition?

- How does this character behave? Consistently? Erratically? Impulsively?
- What sorts of relationships does this character have with other characters in the story? How do others see or react to her or him?
- What are the character's strengths or virtues?
- What are the character's weaknesses or flaws?
- How large a role does this character play in the text? Is she a major character or a minor character? Might he be the protagonist (hero) or the antagonist (villain)?
- Is this character richly rendered (round) or two-dimensional (flat, stock, or stereotype)?
- Does this character change over the course of the narrative (dynamic) or stay the same (static)?
- Is there any indication of why this character acts or thinks the way she does?
- Are there other characters who are strikingly similar to or starkly different from this character?
- What is the conflict in this story, and what is the character's relationship to that conflict?
- Most broadly—and perhaps most importantly—how does this character connect to the text's central themes?

By answering questions like these, you will be well prepared to write an essay that makes a clear analytical claim about your character.

Writing About Adaptation

Many literary texts find a second life through adaptation. As a result, one common essay assignment asks students to consider what a given adaptation has to say about the original text. After all, each adaptation reveals a reader at work. When Baz Luhrmann adapts F. Scott Fitzgerald's *The Great Gatsby* into a film, we get a good sense for what Luhrmann thought was most interesting or important in Fitzgerald's novel. Luhrmann's *The Great Gatsby* is, in this regard, an interpretation of Fitzgerald's well-known story. Even as literary texts are adapted to new forms and reach new audiences, they bear the marks of previous readers and their interpretations. As a result, adapted texts always retain some measure of their "literariness."

Although the most familiar mode of adaptation is that of film adaptation—Hollywood returns to American literature again and again for new ideas—adaptation can take many unusual forms as well: poems become songs, stories become musicals, novels become graphic novels. Some texts even give rise to multiple adaptations, across multiple media. To take one famous example, Herman Melville's *Moby-Dick* has been adapted as a play, an opera, a water ballet, a Hanna-Barbera cartoon, a performance piece by Laurie Anderson, and an album by the progressive metal band Mastodon.

A writing assignment about an adapted work typically takes the form of a compare/contrast essay, in which you compare a literary text to its adaptation. As with any comparison assignment, you want to avoid merely cataloging similarities and differences between the text and its adaptation. (Such a laundry list will not be terribly interesting—for you or for your reader.) Instead, you should try to examine the significance of the similarities and differences you have observed. Why do those similarities and differences matter?

As you begin to take notes on the adaptation, be sure to pay particular attention to differences that seem to have been produced by the movement across media or forms. For example, in one of its earliest Halloween specials, *The Simpsons* adapted Edgar Allan Poe's 1845 poem "The Raven." In this six-minute sketch, the poem is read by the actor James Earl Jones. What effect does Jones's booming baritone have on your impression of the poem? How does his voice interact with the visuals that accompany the reading? Since this is a cartoon adaptation, the creators of *The Simpsons* could add a visual aspect to the poem that Poe could not. What do the often-comical animations add to the poem?

In addition to differences, you should also pay close attention to similarities. For every "D'oh," "Eat my shorts," and "Why you . . . ," *The Simpsons'* adaptation of "The Raven" offers a nearly complete recitation of the poem. Why might the adapters have remained so faithful to the original text? What is the effect of having so much Poe in this sketch? Does the adaptation capture something fundamental about the poem? If so, what?

Once you have identified the differences and similarities between the works at hand, you will want to ask yourself two key questions. First, what seems to be the purpose of this adaptation? Is it merely trying to reach a new or different audience? Or does the adaptation change or update the message of the original text? Remember: successful adaptation essays always articulate clearly what a given adaptation is trying to accomplish. Second, what does this adaptation suggest about the adapters' understanding or interpretation of the original text? How and where can we see the marks of their imaginative encounter with the author? Most broadly, what sort of readers are these adapters?

The list of adaptations you could write about is impossibly long—especially given that some adaptations offer very free interpretations. Many do not use the same title as the original work, and some are adaptations in only the loosest sense of the word. For instance, during the 1950s and 1960s the director Roger Corman made eight campy film adaptations of Poe's stories and poems, nearly all of which bear only the slightest resemblance to the original texts. Similarly, some modern versions of older works are not adaptations per se but, rather, retellings of the earlier texts. For instance, the teen comedy *Easy A* (2010) is a retelling of Nathaniel Hawthorne's *The Scarlet Letter* (1850) as set in a modern-day high school. With a knowing wink, the film shows the students reading *The Scarlet Letter* and watching its earlier film adaptations.

As this suggests, almost all adaptations involve a process of significant contraction or expansion. E. Annie Proulx's short story "Brokeback Mountain" was a mere thirty pages long when it was published in 1997. Yet Ang Lee's 2005 film version clocked in at nearly two hours fifteen minutes. Again, because adapters are interpreters first, we can read their contractions and expansions as evidence of their imaginative engagement with the original text.

Writing About Movies, Music, and Other Media

As the above suggests, some American literature courses use a very broad definition of "literature." Many instructors teach American film and popular music alongside fiction, poetry, and oratory. As a student in such a course, you may feel a bit daunted or overwhelmed by this multidisciplinary mixing. And with good reason: film studies and musicology have their own respective vocabularies and conventions. (Indeed, film studies even has its own *Writing About . . .* guide, *Writing About Movies*. This speaks to both the highly specialized language of film and the fact that literature and film are often taught together.) But breathe easy: if you are encountering film, music, visual art, video games, or other media in an American literature classroom, then most likely the instructor wants you to treat these texts in literary ways. That is, unless your instructor tells you otherwise, you should approach these nonliterary texts with many of the same tools and techniques that you would a piece of fiction or poetry. Textual, contextual, and comparative analyses are just as valid for a video game as they are for a villanelle. When instructors assign, say, a Bob Dylan song or a Kara Walker print or a Levi's commercial, they are likely not asking you to be an expert in music theory or woodcutting or advertising. Instead, they are encouraging you to see connections between literature, other arts, and the broader world.

Essay Exams

Not every assignment for your American literature course will involve writing a paper. In fact, not all American literature courses have formal writing requirements per se. Many courses use in-class "essay exams," where students are expected to write a short essay, in class, during a timed examination period. Most of the advice in this book applies to essay exams, but you may need to make a few adjustments to your writing process.

There are two important differences between an essay exam and a standard, take-home essay assignment: you likely will not be able to do any additional research or use any outside sources, and you will certainly have a time limit during the examination. These differences require a slightly different approach to writing.

First, you need to consider the type of essay you are being asked to write. It is therefore crucial that you take the time to carefully read the prompt. Examinations often produce anxiety for students. Try as hard as you can to stay calm and focus on the actual words on the examination. Ask yourself the following questions: What exactly am I being asked to do here? Have I read all of the instructions? Is there any "fine print"?

In some cases your instructor might give a specific essay prompt on an exam, one that asks you to do a specific thing with a specific text or a small set of texts. Alternatively, you might receive an intentionally broad prompt, one that asks you to come up with your own topic based on your own choice of texts. Take a moment to look back at the kinds of writing assignments described earlier in this guide. You will notice that some types of papers lend themselves to in-class writing better than others. For instance, textual analysis works quite well in an examination setting, in no small part because all it requires is your memory and knowledge of the primary text. Comparative analysis is also a reasonable approach for an essay exam; after all, you will almost certainly have a strong working knowledge of more than one primary text that you have read for the class. (At the risk of betraying a professional secret, college instructors often love to assign comparative prompts for essay exams. This makes sense because comparative analysis requires students to be responsible for multiple texts from a syllabus.)

Contextual analysis might also work, but remember that you likely will not have access to additional research or outside sources. As a result, you will be limited to the knowledge of history, culture, or other relevant information that you have when you enter the examination. However, if you happen to know a lot about, for instance, the American Civil War, and your final examination asks you to talk about Walt Whitman and Emily Dickinson, then you're in luck! You already have the tools to incorporate historical context into your essay.

Except in unusual circumstances, writing about adaptation is probably not a good idea in an essay exam—unless the prompt asks you to do so explicitly. Reading (or viewing, or listening to) the adapted form of a work is essentially a form of research, which you simply will not have the time to do during the examination. Unless you have an exceptionally strong knowledge of, for example, a film version of the primary text about which you are writing, it is probably best to choose a different approach.

The most important factor to consider with essay exams is the time limit, which should affect your preparatory work. You have two goals for your in-class prep work: do it quickly, and make it effective. This strategy will allow you to spend the majority of your time actually writing your essay. Needless to say, when you are in a timed environment, you do not want to spend too much time generating and organizing your ideas. If you do, then you run the risk of not having enough time to finish the essay. On the other hand, you do not want to jump right into the essay without any forethought. If you perform your preparatory work well, then it should make the essay-writing process go much faster.

In Chapter 3 we will present some techniques for generating ideas: brainstorming, freewriting, a discovery draft, five Ws and an H, and so on. If you are taking a course in which the essay exam is the primary writing requirement, then read the descriptions of these idea-generating techniques with a critical eye. Some of these techniques are more useful for essay exams than others, mostly because of how long they will take to perform. Brainstorming (page 49), for example, can be done fairly quickly, so it is a good strategy for an essay exam. The journalistic five Ws and an H technique (page 54) is also relatively quick, and it has the benefit of giving you a specific writing goal. Even tagmemics (page 55) or a very brief run through the topoi (page 57) could prove useful. Suffice it to say, you should use whichever method you have found to be efficient.

After you come up with some ideas, it might be tempting to start writing—after all, the clock is ticking! But you should resist that temptation, at least for a little while. On an essay exam you need more than just an idea; you also need a plan. A crucial step is to take the ideas from your brainstorming or other prewriting exercises and organize them into a coherent outline. Because the exercise is timed, you needn't produce something fancy or overly detailed. Just make a quick sketch of how the essay will take shape. With the outline to guide you, the writing process should go much more smoothly.

More to the point, the outline will almost certainly make the essay clearer and more coherent—and, thus, better.

Keep in mind that even though in-class writing and essay exams will *feel* different from regular essay assignments, in truth this form of writing is different in degree, not kind. The pieces of advice you will read in this book—about developing your thesis, organizing your argument, arranging your paragraphs, and making your essay coherent—all still apply to essay exams.

One final note: on an essay examination, it is often a good idea to plan out how you will spend your time—down to the minute. Let's suppose you have a midterm examination in a fifty-minute class session. The instructor gives you three prompts and tells you to choose one. Your plan for the exam might look like this:

2 minutes: think about the prompts and choose one

5 minutes: brainstorm

7 minutes: nutshell from the brainstorm; come up with a working thesis

7 minutes: create a detailed outline

25 minutes: write the essay

4 minutes: reread what you have written and make revisions

Whatever schedule you create, make sure you dedicate enough time to preparatory work and outlining. This preparatory work will make the essay easier to write—and will result in a better product.

In some instances, completing detailed preparatory work may also have a hidden benefit. If you unfortunately run out of time before completing the essay, your brainstorming notes and outline may help show your instructor what you would have written if the examination period had been longer. We aren't suggesting that your instructor will give partial credit for a good outline, but providing such an outline can certainly demonstrate that you have read and understood the material and that you have something to say.

Creative Prompts

Occasionally an instructor will ask you for a bit of creativity in an assignment. For instance, students might be asked to write a fixed verse poem and then to reflect on what the exercise taught them about poetic form. Another common creative prompt asks students to rewrite the ending of a story, or to imagine what happens next to a story's characters. For instance, your instructor might ask you to rewrite the ending of Kate Chopin's *The Awakening,* since its final scene leaves a great deal unresolved—for both Edna and the people from whom she swims away.

In responding to such creative prompts, you should remember that your instructor is likely much more interested in your creative process than in your creative product. Think of creative prompts as just another opportunity to show off your critical understanding of the text. And if your rewriting or continuation of *The Awakening* does not live up to Chopin's lyrical prose, do not fret. Most often, the instructor just wants to see that you engaged the assignment in an earnest and thoroughgoing way.

3

Generating Ideas

I n some ways writing about literature is similar to writing about any subject: you must choose a topic, generate ideas, do research, craft a thesis, structure your argument, and find the proper tone. But each of these general steps requires you to perform tasks that are specific to the study of American literature. The following chapters combine general advice with suggestions specific to the study of American literature, with the aim of helping you to produce better papers for your American literature class.

But before we go any further we need to discuss two reading practices that will prepare you for success in your American literature course.

Reading Critically / Reading Creatively

As we have said earlier, literature is a social phenomenon. However, the act of reading is usually an individual pursuit.

While there are many advantages to the individual nature of reading—for example, you can read at your own pace, wherever and whenever you like—there are some disadvantages as well. When you have social interactions with other people, your communication involves much more than just words; hand gestures, facial expressions, tone of voice, and other behaviors help to convey meaning. When you read, however, you do not have the benefit of that additional, nonverbal information. Authors therefore use other techniques to help convey their meaning. It is your job as a reader to identify and decipher the "clues" the author leaves for you. This requires you to read both *critically* and *creatively*. It also requires you to read methodically. The most successful students and scholars of American literature are those who read slowly, carefully, and repeatedly—again and again, if need be—until they feel that all of the text's possible meanings are in hand.

READING CRITICALLY

Critical reading involves looking beyond what a text *says* to discover what it *means*. This reading practice begins with the understanding that the words you see on the page are only a starting point, and that other information is available to you. First and foremost, you should examine the *way* those words are presented, as well as the *choices* the author makes in crafting the text: language and tone, figures of speech, humor, rhythm, and so on. You should also try to determine what purpose these textual elements serve. Here are two examples of critical reading in practice.

Mark Twain's *Adventures of Huckleberry Finn* opens with a famous word of caution to readers: "NOTICE / Persons attempting to find a motive in this narrative will be prosecuted; persons attempting to find a moral in it will be banished; persons attempting to find a plot in it will be shot. / BY ORDER OF THE AUTHOR / Per G.G., CHIEF OF ORDNANCE." Read literally, this sentence suggests that the subsequent novel is without motive, moral, or plot. "Excellent," the uncritical reader might say, "I can just read this for fun." However, if you read the text a little more closely, there are key clues to suggest that the author may not mean exactly what he says, and that this book should in fact be read for motive, moral, and plot.

First, we might note the out-of-place nature of the "Notice," which seems like something you might find at the door of a nineteenth-century tavern rather than in the opening pages of a nineteenth-century novel. Second, the tone of the notice seems to get increasingly agitated as we move from threats of prosecution to threats of banishment and even execution. Third, that growing agitation reaches its apex with the declaration "persons attempting to find a plot in it will be shot." The rhyming of "plot" and "shot" might suggest that Twain is having some fun at our expense. At the very least, the rhyme introduces some levity into an otherwise deadly serious notice. But the literal meaning of this sentence is also a bit absurd. A novel may not have a clear motive or definitive moral message, but it typically has a plot. Finally, we might ask, who is this "G.G., CHIEF OF ORDNANCE," anyway?

Even if you knew nothing about Mark Twain's reputation as a deeply ironic writer, all these clues suggest that something complicated (and potentially comical) is going on here. Critical reading is therefore in order. Although Twain's meaning may not be entirely clear here—or elsewhere in *Huck Finn*, for that matter—this ironic notice introduces us to the novel's odd blend of humor and high seriousness. In this way the irony of the passage provides a key to help you read the rest of the work. You now know that the author provides information ironically. You should read accordingly—which is to say *critically*.

Even when they aren't being ironic, authors will very often provide information about characters or events via clues that you must decipher. For instance, Edgar Allan Poe's narrators are often "mad"; that is, they suffer from some sort of mental illness that makes them highly unreliable narrators. Look at the opening paragraphs of any of the following texts: "The Raven," "Annabel Lee," "Ligeia," "The Man of the Crowd," "The Tell-Tale Heart," "The Black Cat," "The Cask of Amontillado." At what point do you question the narrator's sanity or reliability? How does Poe accomplish this effect? Here are the first two sentences of "The Tell-Tale Heart": "True!—nervous— very, very dreadfully nervous I had been, and am; but why *will* you say that I am mad? The disease had sharpened my senses—not destroyed—not dulled them." Why would Poe break up these sentences in this way? What are we supposed to infer about the narrator from such fragmentation?

READING CREATIVELY

Creative reading involves trying to fully occupy the world that the text imagines in order to better understand its abstract ideas and broader themes. This reading practice begins with the understanding that reading literature is a profoundly imaginative act. Each reader makes the text at hand come alive (or wither and die) as he or she imagines specific aspects of a work's setting, characterization, tone, and the like. In imagining, for instance, the sound of a character's voice or the smell of a particular room, the reader comes to collaborate with the writer. Here are two examples of creative reading in practice.

Ralph Ellison's *Invisible Man* offers one of the most vivid and troubling imaginative worlds in all of American literature. Take, for instance, the opening scene of the novel. It is one thing to read Ellison's description of the Invisible Man's lair; it is quite another to imagine what it would be like to live underground, in a "warm hole" in a basement with "exactly 1,369 lights." Our narrator notes:

> I've wired the entire ceiling, every inch of it. And not with fluorescent bulbs, but with the older, more-expensive-to-operate kind, the filament type. An act of sabotage, you know. I've already begun to wire the wall. A junk man

I know, a man of vision, has supplied me with wire and sockets. Nothing, storm or flood, must get in the way of our need for light and ever more and brighter light. The truth is the light and light is the truth. When I finish all four walls, then I'll start on the floor.

As the reader begins to picture this brilliant scene in her or his mind, Ellison's words give rise to specific, even idiosyncratic mental images. They also raise a number of questions: Wouldn't it get hot down there with all those lights? Is there a constant buzzing or a smell of filaments burning? Can you see clearly with that much light? Such questions address nearly all of the senses. (The fifth sense, taste, is addressed later in the prologue as the Invisible Man eats vanilla ice cream with sloe gin.) In imagining this fantastical scene, the reader has a virtual or vicarious experience of the Invisible Man's world. This, in turn, allows that reader to better understand a character who "feels so black and blue," as well as a novel that insists on the bright light of truth.

As these examples suggest, it is often difficult to get at the broader meaning of a text without fully immersing oneself in the world of that text. And some worlds will be harder for you to imagine than others. This challenge is particularly evident when you encounter texts from regions or time periods you don't know much about. In reading, for instance, *A Narrative of the Captivity and Restoration of Mrs. Mary Rowlandson* (1682) students often struggle to understand Rowlandson's actions, emotions, and motivations during her captivity. To be sure, hers is a conflicted and complex narrative. But the historical and cultural differences between the seventeenth-century Massachusetts Bay Colony and, say, the twenty-first-century United States are profound—and often profoundly alienating for students. Even the most imaginative reader struggles to immerse herself or himself in Rowlandson's world.

Fortunately, there are spurs to imaginative reading. A little background information about the historical and cultural contexts of the narrative will help you to better imagine—and thus better understand—Mary Rowlandson's various "removes" and restoration. Such an investigation doesn't have to involve extensive, time-consuming research. You might start by gathering any information that will help you to create a mental picture of the scenes the text describes: *How would Mary Rowlandson and her captors have dressed?* (Fashion choices might be different for wealthy characters than for poor characters, or they might differ due to the characters' jobs, social standing, and so on.) *How did people in these societies talk?* (Consider the language the characters are speaking, as well as the patterns and habits of discourse they exhibit.) *What was normal behavior in both the Colony and camps?* (Investigate dominant social values or mores. Consider whether characters act in accordance with those values or whether they violate them.) Questions like these will help you to occupy more fully Mary Rowlandson's world.

Generating Ideas

By reading a work of literature critically and creatively, you will usually come up with some ideas worth writing about. But what if you have read the work a few times and still haven't found anything that you feel is worth exploring? Or what if you have found an idea worth writing about but don't know how to develop it? The following strategies for generating ideas can help get you writing.

CONVERSATION

After experiencing a cultural event like a movie or concert, we typically talk about it with others—sometimes just as soon as we leave the venue. Those conversations often leave us thinking about the movie or concert in new and interesting ways. Similarly, conversations with your classmates about works of literature can help you to discover what you find compelling in a particular work. Of course it is worth noting that the kinds of conversations we have with our friends—which are often freewheeling, opinionated, and emotional—mark just the beginning of scholarly inquiry. Nonetheless, talking with friends about the texts in your American literature course can assist you in exploring differences of opinion, and in articulating and supporting your point of view.

BRAINSTORMING

Another way to formulate ideas is to brainstorm. Brainstorming is useful because it is a quick and efficient way of laying out what you know about a subject. Brainstorming can also help you to see what you do not know about a subject. This, in turn, might encourage you to read and think more deeply about the subject.

Suppose you have decided to brainstorm for a paper on Walt Whitman's poem "Song of Myself." You might make a list like the one that follows:

"Song of Myself"
- marked a revolution in American poetry;
- doesn't rhyme;
- includes many lists;
- talks a lot about the different people the speaker meets;
- talks a lot about the speaker;
- celebrates the human body in great detail;
- begins with the word "I" and ends with the word "you";
- was published with a prose preface that argued for a certain type of American poetry and a certain type of American poet.

As this list illustrates, brainstorming is an informal strategy for invention in which you jot down, as quickly as you can, ideas concerning your topic. The ideas do not have to be connected—though sometimes looking for connections will yield a paper topic. For instance, beginning with this list of ideas, you might end up writing a paper arguing that "Song of Myself" is a poem that self-consciously breaks from previous American poetry in order to celebrate the diversity of the country and its people.

Remember that you can also stop at any point in the writing process to brainstorm, especially when you feel that you are stuck or have gaps to fill in your argument. Again, when you brainstorm you freely explore your topic without the pressure of structure, grammar, or style. In the process, ideas for an essay (or a paragraph, or even a footnote) can evolve unhindered.

FREEWRITING

Freewriting is similar to brainstorming in that it is a quick and informal way to develop an idea. But whereas brainstorming often takes the form of a list, freewriting involves prose. In freewriting, you elaborate on your ideas, without paying attention to syntax or grammar.

Here is an example of freewriting:

> OK, so I just finished T.S. Eliot's The Wasteland and, wow, I'm supposed to write a paper on it but I have no idea what I'm going to say. It was super hard to make sense of; half the time I was wondering what the heck was the point of

all the different shifts in tone and topic. It felt like a bunch of people were talking at the same time. Prof said that the original title was "he does the police in different voices." (look this up.) but still i gotta come up with something. where to start? maybe i should begin by focusing on the first section, which made the most sense to me.

I also think there might be some funny moments I could talk about, like when he says "Madame Sosostris, famous clairvoyante, Had a bad cold." I mean the poem is pretty depressing. "April is the cruelest month, breeding" etc. But it's also funny at times, in a dark way, but still funny. lots of the humor is about words and what they mean. Other words just seem made up. Maybe there's something to say about how language sounds rather than how language means? Datta. Dayadhvam. Damyata. Shantih shantih shanith. Sounds like nonesense to me but those footnotes say they're from Hindu. Maybe say something about foreign language and translation?

Oh and I liked the bit about the "unreal city." That's cool. It shows up a couple of times. I wonder where this is all supposed to be taking place. London maybe? Somewhere else? I think London must be the unreal city. Why is that important.

So maybe I can write about something here? Voices. Funny, nonsense language. The unreal city. hmmmm. We'll see. . . .

In most cases, freewriting is intended for the writer's eyes only. That may help to explain the various spelling, grammatical, and typographical errors above. It is also okay for a freewrite to be a bit disjointed or all over the place. Although the writing is scattered, the student above has accomplished a great deal in a very short space. He has identified at least three potential topics for further development—humor, foreign phrases, and the image of the "unreal city" in "The Wasteland"—any of which might result in a strong paper.

DISCOVERY DRAFT

A discovery draft is another strategy for coming up with or developing your ideas. A discovery draft is similar to freewriting in that you can write freely, with little thought to matters of style. However, writing a discovery draft is different from freewriting in that a discovery draft makes a conscious attempt to focus on and develop an idea or a cluster of ideas. In other words, a discovery draft is freewriting with an agenda. And because you have an agenda, a discovery draft tends to be more structured than freewriting; it also tends to be written more or less coherently, in complete sentences.

Think of writing a discovery draft as writing a letter to a friend about your paper. Suppose you have just read Louise Erdrich's poem "Dear John Wayne." You might first summarize, for your friend's benefit, the poem and the issues it presents. You might then raise questions about the work. You might challenge the author on certain points. You might point out a certain part of the work that you found particularly compelling. You might address and then work out any confusion that you have about specific phrases or the poem's broader meaning. In writing the discovery draft you might also have an "aha! moment" in which you see something you hadn't seen before and break off midsentence to explore it.

In a sense, the aha! moment is the point of the discovery draft. When writing the discovery draft, your thoughts are focused on your topic. You are giving language to your questions and observations. In this process, the mind almost always stumbles across something new—it makes a discovery. And with this discovery, a successful paper is often launched.

Creating a discovery draft is more formal than a freewriting exercise. It always uses complete sentences and correct grammar, and, most importantly, it follows a logical train of thought. However, it is still not nearly as formal as a paper that you would hand in to your instructor. It uses casual, even colloquial language, and it does not state ideas as strongly as it might. (This is because in a discovery draft you are still trying to figure out what, exactly, those ideas are.) It also typically uses some of the thoughts that showed up in the freewrite. Freewriting helps you find ideas that might be useful in your paper; the discovery draft helps you figure out how these ideas are useful and what you might say about them. A student who takes the time to do both a freewriting exercise and a discovery draft will be well on the way to a solid working thesis.

FIVE *WS* AND AN *H*

Journalism has provided us with perhaps the simplest and most familiar way of coming up with a topic: simply ask questions such as *who*, *what*, *when*, *where*, *why*, and *how*. Answering these questions doesn't seem very hard at first—until one gets to the *why* and *how*. Then things get tricky.

Let's use this method to try to generate ideas for a paper on Henry David Thoreau's *Walden*. Maybe when you were reading the narrative you got interested in Thoreau's quotation of poetry in the text, so you have a topic you want to explore. Now begin your interrogation by asking the following:

Where in the narrative do you find poetry? Mark the
sections.

What are the poems that Thoreau quotes? Write down the
title of each poem.

How are the poems presented? Using your footnotes and the
Internet, track down the full text of each poem. How
much of a given poem does Thoreau quote? Which
poems get fully reproduced? Which get excerpted?

Who are the poets he quotes? Again, using the resources
available to you, find out a bit more about each of the
poets he quotes. Are there any patterns here? Where
are these poets from? When were they born? What
were their politics?

When in the narrative does poetry appear? What is happening in those moments? What purpose does the poetry

seem to serve at each particular moment? How does the poem comment on the rest of the scene, or on the narrative as a whole?

After thinking about the answers to these questions, ask yourself: *Why does poetry play such a prominent role in* Walden?

The last question is, admittedly, a tough one. But it is precisely when you have difficulty answering a *why* question that a real paper is beginning to emerge. When the answer comes too easily, you are on familiar ground, so you are probably not saying anything all that interesting or original. Cultivate a taste for confusion. And then cultivate a strategy for clearing up confusion. Only when you ask a question that initially confuses you can real thinking and real writing begin.

TAGMEMICS

Tagmemics is a system that allows you to look at a single object from three different perspectives. One of these perspectives (or even all three) can help you determine a subject for writing. By extending an analogy regarding the different ways physicists think about light, tagmemics involves seeing your topic

as a particle (as a thing in itself);
as a wave (as a thing changing over time);
as part of a field (as a thing in its context).

Suppose you want to write a paper on Henry James's "The Beast in the Jungle." If you use tagmemics as a system of invention, you will begin by looking at the story as a thing in itself. In other words, you will do a close textual analysis, paying attention to the words on the page and the implications those words have for your interpretation of the story.

Next you might consider how the story has changed over time. How was "The Beast in the Jungle" received in its day? How does this reception compare to current assessments of the story? Research notable criticism of the story, such as that by Leon Edel, Eve Kosofsky Sedgwick, and J. Hillis Miller. Which elements of the story have critics been interested in, and at what point in time? How has the approach to James's story changed over time?

Finally, consider "The Beast in the Jungle" as a thing in context. Relate it to its culture and its moment in time. James wrote the story in the first years of the twentieth century. What was happening in his life in the early 1900s? What was happening in the world in the early 1900s? Even unlikely events or historical facts may provide a compelling context. For instance, many critics have noted that by the early 1900s James was more or less a "confirmed bachelor." Might this connect with the "essential loneliness" of the story's main character, John Marcher? More broadly, the end of the nineteenth century had produced a good deal of anxiety about the decadence and degeneration of life in Europe. How might this story be commenting on this anxiety?

ARISTOTLE'S TOPOI

As one of the fathers of rhetoric, Aristotle worked to formalize a system for conceiving, organizing, and expressing ideas. His "topoi"—a system of specific strategies for invention—are particularly useful for academic writing. Think of the topoi as a series of questions that you might ask of a work of literature—questions that might lead you to compelling paper topics. The topoi are especially helpful when you are asked to explore a topic that seems very broad. Consider, for instance, how using the topoi can help you write a paper on the importance of Emily Dickinson to twentieth-century experimental poetry.

Use definition

You can use definition in two ways to come up with or develop a topic. First you might look at *genus*, which Aristotle explains as defining a general idea within specific limits. For example, you could define "twentieth-century experimental poetry" with the intent of showing how Dickinson's poetry anticipates certain elements of later experimental poetry.

The second way to use definition is to think in terms of *division*. In other words, try to think of your subject in terms of its parts. For example, identify the aspects of Dickinson's poetry that are most significant with regard to poetic experimentation, or with regard to other well-known works by experimental poets.

Use comparison

You can generate ideas by making comparisons in two ways. The first is to look for *similarities* and/or *differences*. For example, you might determine how Dickinson's poetry stands apart from that of other important nineteenth-century poets such as Walt Whitman.

The second method is to compare *degree*. In other words, you might consider how something is more or less (or better or worse) than something else. For example, is Dickinson's poetry a better representation of experimental poetry than Whitman's poetry? Why or why not? Are there other poets who had a greater influence on twentieth-century experimental poetry?

Explore relationships

Aristotle determined four ways of exploring relationships as a strategy for coming up with ideas for writing. The first is to consider either the *cause* of your subject or its *effects*. For example, you might research the effects that Dickinson's poetry had on subsequent poetry, experimental or otherwise.

Second, you might consider a subject's *antecedents* and *consequences*. In other words, you might ask this question of your subject: If this, then what? For example, if Dickinson's poetry had never been discovered, would American poetry look any different today?

Third, you might examine *contraries*, or make an argument by proving its opposite. An example is to say that war is bad in order to convey the idea that peace is good. Along these lines, you might argue that Dickinson's poetry was influential by showing how that of other nineteenth-century poets was not.

Finally, you might look for *contradictions, incompatible statements,* or *controversy.* For example, some critics feel that Dickinson wrote some of the greatest poems of the nineteenth century; others feel that her poetry is overrated, too confusing, or too abstract. You can explore the controversy and stake a claim of your own.

Examine circumstances

In seeking an idea for a paper, you can examine circumstances in two ways. The first is to consider the possible and the impossible. Sometimes you can construct an original argument by considering what is possible and what is not. For example, imagine if Dickinson had submitted more of her poems for publication during her lifetime. How might editors have shaped her irregular verse into more conservative forms?

The second strategy is to consider the past or look to the future. For example, in what ways was her work influenced by the long history of poetry, and in what ways does it diverge from that history? In what ways does Dickinson influence poets (or other writers) working today? Given current trends in poetry and poetics, how might her influence carry on into the mid-twenty-first century?

Rely on testimony

The opinions of others can also be a source for your paper. Look to authorities, testimonials, statistics, maxims, laws, and precedents. For example, you might read what critics have to say about Dickinson's idiosyncratic use of dashes or adaptations of the common or hymn meter. Alternatively, you might think about what her poetry's ongoing popularity tells us about her influence on later poets.

Developing Your Ideas

So you have done some preliminary brainstorming. Perhaps you have even completed a discovery draft. The problem now is that you have too many ideas and you don't know what to do with them. Or perhaps the ideas you have come up with don't seem adequately academic. What do you do next?

NUTSHELLING

Nutshelling is the simple process of trying to explain the main point of your observations in a few sentences—in a nutshell, that is. When you put your thoughts in a nutshell, you come to see just how those thoughts fit together. You also see how each thought is relevant to the others, and gain a better sense for your overall point. As with a discovery draft, you should write in complete sentences. Indeed, formal writing is now a must, since much of the language of your nutshell may be later imported into your paper. If done right, nutshelling helps you transform your observations into something meaningful, focused, and coherent. It also gives you a promising plan for the introduction of your paper.

BROADENING YOUR TOPIC

What happens when you have put your thoughts in a nutshell but they seem too "small"? You may have come up with a topic that is too narrow or too particular to support a sustained conversation.

Suppose your assignment is to write a paper on Flannery O'Connor's "Good Country People." As you read, you notice that the names of the characters seem to be ironic. You decide that this is a good topic to explore further for your paper.

You take notes about all of the names in the story: Mrs. Hopewell, Mrs. Freeman, Joy (who renames herself Hulga), and Manley Pointer (whose real name is never given). You note that Mrs. Hopewell is not actually all that hopeful, Mrs. Freeman is a tenant farmer, and Joy is utterly joyless; this is to say nothing of the fact that Manley Pointer is a rather suggestive name for a bible salesman. So far, so good: you have made a very promising observation.

But, alas, the observation still isn't "big" enough. Why not? Because it remains an observation, not an argument. You have identified an important pattern in the story, but you haven't said why that pattern is significant. What is O'Connor doing here with names? How do you broaden your topic—from observation to idea—so that you have something important to say?

First, you should try to make connections. Are there other ironic aspects of the story? Can you find other instances where a character seems to say one thing but mean the opposite? What are we to make of the fact that both Manley Pointer and Joy-Hulga change their names? And what exactly does Pointer keep in his bible?

Second, turn your idea inside out. Are there any characters in the story who are truly straightforward—who say what they mean and mean what they say? At one point Joy-Hulga says, "There mustn't be anything dishonest between us." Is anyone in this story truly honest?

Third, consider the context. There are, of course, at least two contexts to consider: the context within the story and the context without. Within the story, you might seek a context for O'Connor's use of names. What might O'Connor be signaling through her ironic use of names? What does the author seem to think about the characters in this story? What is the broader theme of this story about "good country people"?

Without the story are other contexts. Consider, for instance, O'Connor's other stories. How does she use names elsewhere? The lead character in "The Life You Save May Be Your Own" is the rather shiftless Mr. Shiftlet. More broadly, this story was published in 1955, during a period in which the U.S. South was under increasing scrutiny for its poverty and racial unrest.

How might O'Connor be sending up the idea of "good country people"—in the South and beyond?

All of these questions might help you to broaden your topic, tie your observations to bigger questions, and make your paper more substantial and interesting.

NARROWING/FOCUSING YOUR TOPIC

What if your topic seems too big to handle? What do you do then?

Let's continue thinking about the hypothetical paper on Flannery O'Connor's "Good Country People." Perhaps after brainstorming and freewriting, you have concluded that none of the characters in the story are quite what they seem. This observation is a good start, but you should resist the temptation to be satisfied with it. Simply stating that O'Connor's characters are not particularly honest or have ulterior motives is not enough. A paper showing how Mrs. Freeman is dishonest and Mrs. Hopewell is dishonest and Joy-Hulga is dishonest will probably bore your reader. "Okay," the reader might say, "these are dishonest characters—so what?" Now you need to focus your topic so that your observation can be extended to an interesting and significant conclusion. How do you focus your topic?

First, test your claim. A statement as broad as this one is probably not always true. Are any of the characters in the story what they seem? Is anyone straightforward and honest? Better yet, are there *degrees* of straightforwardness and honesty in the story? If so, how do you account for that evidence while still defending your claim? For instance, what are we to do with Joy-Hulga's declaration that "there mustn't be anything dishonest" between herself and Manley Pointer? Why does she seem to value frankness and honesty at this moment in the text? In every paper you write, you need to address any parts of the text that might challenge your central claim. This will help you move from a broad to a specific topic; it will also give rise to more nuanced claims.

Next look for *specific* examples in the text. Specific examples, rather than broad information, will make your topic clearer; they will also help you present your argument in a compelling fashion. For instance, you might look at the opening paragraph of the story. We are told that Mrs. Freeman "could never be brought to admit herself wrong on any point." Where does this characterization place her on an honest-dishonest continuum? Why do you think O'Connor would open "Good Country People" with a description of Mrs. Freeman's reluctance to admit she is wrong? Once you have found evidence to support your point, go back and look for more. Since these examples will likely make up the majority of your paper, it is important to be thorough. It is also important to be detailed. Whenever you can, quote directly from the text.

Finally, consider the context. Just as a consideration of context can help you to broaden an idea, it can also help you to focus it. We know that O'Connor included ironic character names in many of her stories. Is there something different or particularly striking about her use of names here? Does the historical or regional context of the story provide any clue as to why O'Connor pushes so hard on the idea that "You don't see any more real honest people unless you go way out in the country"?

Essentially, you are looking for details that support your specific claim while simultaneously sifting out the parts of the story that are not important to your argument. If you fail to go through that sifting process, you may end up including extraneous information in your essay, and your instructor will likely tell you that the paper seems disorganized. If you do a good job of narrowing your focus, organization should not be a problem.

Thinking Beyond the Page

So far, we've been advising you to consider the formal aspects of the literature that you are writing about—the literature as it is rendered on the page. Sometimes, however, you will want to "think beyond the page" and consider questions about how the work was originally composed, its historical context, and so on. For example, ask yourself the following questions:

What do you know about the author? Learn more about the life and career of the author. If you have some sense of his or her other works, you will have a better understanding of the themes and genres that interest the author.

What is the composition and publication history of this work? See if you can discover anything about the conditions under which the work was produced. You might find that the author produced multiple, significantly different versions of the text. Or you might discover that the version of a text we know looked radically different when it was first published. For instance, three of William Carlos Williams's most famous poems, "Spring and All," "To Elsie," and "The Red Wheelbarrow," first appeared as untitled parts of a landmark volume of mixed prose and poetry called *Spring and All*. What is it like to read these poems in their original context, alongside Williams's prose sketches and manifestos?

You might also discover that a text was first published in a periodical. This method of publication is quite common for poems and short stories, and many novels were first published serially in magazines or newspapers. If you discover significant differences between the periodical publication and the book publication, you might want to investigate what led to those changes. Was there a controversy over the text's content? Or were the changes perhaps due to demands of the marketplace? In any case, examining multiple versions of the same work can provide you with a lot of interesting information that you can use for a paper.

What do the critics and scholars say? Reading what others have said about the work before you read it can also help you focus your observations. If a work is particularly well known for its innovative approach to rendering characters' inner lives (Charlotte Perkins Gilman's "The Yellow Wallpaper," for example), you will want to pay close attention to this aspect of the work as you reread it.

Does the work reflect an interesting cultural phenomenon?
Sometimes an instructor will ask you to read certain literary works because she wants you to examine a specific cultural phenomenon. Readers of James Wright's poem "Autumn Begins in Martins Ferry, Ohio" often comment on the sense of community that the football game engenders. As people from all walks of life watch their sons "gallop terribly against each other's bodies," something strange seems to happen. You might use this poem to think about the relationship between sports and community.

Asking these questions may lead you to a promising topic. However, you may also find that you still don't know enough to write your paper. In that case, further research is in order. The next chapter provides some guidance on the research process.

Gocsik & Hutchison
<u>Writing about American Lit.</u>
W.W. Norton & Co., 2014

4

Researching American Literature

Doing research in an American literature class is in many ways similar to doing research for other classes: you will visit the library (in person or virtually), find books and journals, get a sense for the scholarly conversation around your topic, and then offer a critical perspective of your own. One important difference, though, is that when you write about a work of literature, the literary text itself is typically the primary source, with literary criticism (books, journal articles, and so on) serving as secondary sources.

Understanding Primary and Secondary Sources

Primary sources are defined as any text, artifact, photograph, film, or other medium that is the object of scholarly investigation. A *secondary source*, on the other hand, is a work that analyzes, comments on, or otherwise sheds light on the primary source. A source can be primary or secondary, depending on the purpose of your research. For instance, you might write a paper in which the primary source is something other than a literary work (e.g., an author's journal). Or you might write a paper in which a secondary source consists of fictional elements (e.g., a scene that was removed from a novel in an early manuscript stage).

For example, let's return to that hypothetical paper about Emily Dickinson's influence on twentieth-century experimental poetry. You have thought some more about the topic and you think you want to focus your attention on Dickinson's poem "My Life had stood—a Loaded Gun—." You might begin by reading what other people have written about either the poem itself or Dickinson's influence. Adrienne Rich's famous essay "Vesuvius at Home: The Power of Emily Dickinson" does both. In this situation, Dickinson's "My Life had stood—a Loaded Gun—" remains your primary source, and "Vesuvius at Home" is one of your secondary sources.

However, your instructor might assign a paper that is mainly about Rich's essay. In this situation "Vesuvius at Home" is the primary source, and the other sources you find in your research are secondary. In fact, one of those secondary sources could be "My Life had stood—a Loaded Gun—." The key thing to remember here is that in literary studies the majority of your research will involve secondary sources. That is, unless you are being asked to recover a primary source—an underread novel, an unattributed poem, or an uncollected story—from the dustbin of history. But, in general, the vast majority of your sources will be secondary.

Using Sources

Having a strategy for collecting and employing sources is crucially important. No one wants to wander from source to source trying to remember what, precisely, that source argued, or why it mattered in the first place. We therefore offer the following research tips, which we think will help you to become a more effective and efficient researcher.

These steps may at first seem time-consuming. "Why should I stop to summarize a source when I can simply go back to the original?" you might wonder. However, the strategies outlined here will save you time in the long run. The work you do to digest and classify your sources as you do your research will make the writing process much more focused, much more efficient, and much less painful in the end.

SUMMARIZE YOUR SOURCES

Before attempting to use any source in your paper, make sure you understand it. The best way to do this is to summarize the source. In summarizing, you accomplish several things. First, summarizing a source requires you to put someone else's argument in your own words. Some of your secondary sources might use language that puzzles you. When you summarize, you are, in a sense, translating that argument into language that you can understand and work with. Summarizing also helps you to see any aspects of the argument that you aren't quite getting. If you find yourself stumbling as you attempt to summarize, go back to the original source for clarity.

Summarizing also allows you to restate an argument in terms that are relevant to your paper. Most literary criticism that you will encounter is very complex and offers several ideas for consideration. Some of these ideas will be relevant to your topic, while many others will not. When you summarize, you can restate the part of the argument that seems most relevant to the paper you want to write.

Summarizing can also help you organize your source material. If you have used ten sources in a research project, then you have probably taken a lot of notes and gathered several quotations for your paper. This work can amount to pages and pages of text. Summaries can help you to organize these notes by telling you almost at a glance which idea comes from which source. You can also include in your summaries a few of the best quotations from each source.

Finally, summarizing is helpful throughout the research process. This is not something that you should do once at the beginning of your research and then forget about. Every time your understanding of the topic shifts or evolves, take the time to write a brief summary. You will find that putting your thoughts into writing helps you solidify one stage of understanding before progressing to the next.

CATEGORIZE YOUR SOURCES

Once you have summarized your sources, try to place them in various categories. Remember, writing an academic paper is like taking part in a large, ongoing conversation. Although everyone has a particular point of view, it is safe to say that no one is entering the conversation as a lone wolf. That is, everyone is speaking from a certain critical perspective. These perspectives might be classified into different groups.

Categorizing your sources might be as simple as looking for similarities among them. Which sources seem to share a point of view? Which seem to arrive at similar conclusions? You will also discover differences among your sources. Try to define these differences and see if they seem to fall into categories. For example, side A seems to believe X, while side B seems to believe Y. Or, side A attempts to understand the literary work from a feminist perspective, while side B is interested in interpreting the work from a socioeconomic perspective.

Once you have categorized your sources, try to understand what these differences and similarities mean to your argument. Are these categories relevant to the issues you intend to discuss? Where does your own argument fit in? Does the reader need to know about these categories in order for your argument to make sense? Try to articulate these matters as clearly as possible. Again, write a summary of what you think at this point.

INTERROGATE YOUR SOURCES

In most of the papers you will write in college, you will have to do more than just review what other people have said about a topic. You will also be asked to present your own point of view. To do this, you will need to interrogate your sources.

Interrogating your sources doesn't mean that you have to tear them apart. You don't have to search like a bloodhound for the weak spot in an argument; you aren't required to "take on" your source. In general, academic writing needn't be contentious. Instead, you should ask questions of your sources. Initiate a conversation: challenge, probe, rebut, and confirm. Here are some good questions to ask:

Is the writer offering evidence for her claims? Is this evidence sufficient? Why or why not?

Is there something that the writer is overlooking or omitting? If so, is this a matter of carelessness, or does it seem purposeful? Why?

Does the writer's argument seem reasonable? If not, can you locate places where the reasoning seems to break down? Can you identify any logical fallacies?

Is the writer's language appropriate? Does the writer sometimes rely on a lyrical phrase or a passionate claim to cover up a lack of evidence?

What can you determine about the writer's perspective?
Does the writer seem to have any important biases? Does the
writer seem to belong to a particular critical school of thought?
Does the writer's perspective help or hinder the argument she
or he is trying to make? Why?

Where do you stand in relation to the writer? At the end of
the essay, do you give the writer a round of applause? Or are
you booing her or him off the stage? Are you sitting with
your arms crossed, feeling skeptical? You should keep notes
on your personal responses to the source and try to translate
those responses into further comments or questions.

EVALUATE YOUR SOURCES

As the above suggests, secondary sources will be of varying degrees of help as you write. Some sources will prove
immensely helpful, fundamentally changing the way you
think about your primary text and allowing you to advance
your own informed argument. Other sources, not so much.
You should ask yourself the following *evaluative* questions:
How does this source change the way I am thinking? What
does it allow me to do? Is this, finally, useful to me? Questions like these will help you to determine which sources
should play a major role in your paper. Needless to say,
you should ask these questions throughout the research
process. A source that blew your mind on the first reading
may turn out to be pretty humdrum after you have read

other secondary sources. Reevaluate your sources again and again.

Alas, secondary sources will also be of varying degrees of quality. Most academic writing is carefully researched, carefully written, and carefully edited. But, as with any human endeavor, some of it is also sloppy, sloppy, sloppy. This is true of both print and electronic sources.

In evaluating your sources you should ask the following sorts of questions:

- **How did I find this source?** Was it cited by other scholars? Did I get it from my library?
- **Is it a timely source?** Was it published early last year or early in the last century?
- **What else is published in this venue?** Academic writing? Journalism? Opinion pieces?
- **Was this source reviewed and/or edited before it was published?** Reputable sources will often indicate if the material is "peer-reviewed"—that is, vetted by other scholars before publication.
- **Who is responsible for this source?** What are their qualifications? What else have they written? Do they have an academic affiliation?
- **What sources does the source cite?** Other scholarly articles? Or other websites?
- **Are there clear errors**—typographical, grammatical, historical—**that make me question the quality of this source?**

Although there is no magical formula for what makes a good, reliable source, the process of asking these questions will help you to be a more critical researcher. At a moment when we have more information at our fingertips than ever before, research skills are increasingly important.

ANNOTATE YOUR SOURCES

Most scholars find it useful to mark their texts as they read them. Marking your text enables you to enter into a conversation with the author. When you mark a text you are no longer reading passively. Instead, you are reading actively, filling the margins with comments and questions that could blossom into a paper topic down the road. Annotating your texts also ensures that your responses to a source won't get lost. Entire books and dissertations have evolved from notes made in the margins. The ideas for these books and dissertations might have been lost had the writer not taken the time to jot them down.

MAKE YOUR SOURCES WORK FOR YOU

Students often make a grave mistake when they write their first academic papers: overwhelmed by what their sources have to say, they let their papers crumble under the weight of scholarly opinion. In short, first-time academic writers often end up rehashing what has already been said on a topic rather than advancing an informed argument of their own. Such a paper might be informative. It might even be competently written. But it will not fulfill the requirements of a good academic paper. Remember, a good academic paper must be analytical—which is to say it must be critical—and it must present a well-crafted, persuasive, and informed argument.

Well-crafted, persuasive, and informed arguments usually come about when you make your sources work for *you*. There are several ways to ensure that your sources do indeed work for you and do not overwhelm your argument. First, don't go to the library (or even get online) before you have thought about the topic on your own. No doubt your research will have an impact on what you think. Sometimes you might even find that you reverse your opinion because of your research. But if you go to the library before you have given your topic some thought, then you risk jumping on the bandwagon of the first persuasive argument you encounter.

Second, limit your sources to those that are clearly relevant to your topic. It is easy to get lost in the broader scholarly conversation about your subject. It can also be quite exciting, what with all those new ideas and debates. However, you should always keep your bearings, and ask, again and again, "Does this part of the scholarly conversation actually serve my argument?"

Finally, keep track of your evolving understanding of the topic by periodically stopping to summarize. As we said earlier, summarizing your sources makes them much more manageable. If you manage your sources as you go along, you will reduce the risk that they will overwhelm you later.

Keeping Track of Your Sources

During the research process it is very important to keep track of your sources. Nothing is more frustrating than having a great quotation and not remembering where it came from. You should develop a good, consistent system for keeping notes. (In recent years several software companies have developed programs and even apps to help you keep track of your sources. Your college or university may even make some of these tools available to you.)

Every academic discipline requires that you submit a bibliography or list of works cited with your paper. A bibliography should include every work you looked at in your research, even if you didn't quote that source directly. A list of works cited, on the other hand, is just that: a list of works that you quoted, paraphrased, or alluded to in the text of your paper. Both bibliographies and lists of works cited require you to provide information that will make it easier for your reader to find these sources for her- or himself. Consult the *MLA (Modern Language Association) Handbook* for information about how to construct a proper bibliography and/or list of works cited.

Citing Sources

When you write an academic paper, you must cite all the sources that you have used, even if you don't quote them directly. If you fail to cite these sources, you may be charged with plagiarism. Plagiarism—passing off the words and ideas of others as your own—is an academic offense for which there are serious consequences.

We can offer several good reasons not to plagiarize. First, it is very easy to get caught. Your instructors—who have read countless student papers—are keenly aware of the difference between professional and student writing. They notice when sophisticated, highly polished academic writing appears out of the blue, without development or context. In addition, although the Internet makes plagiarism easy, it also empowers teachers, who can utilize sophisticated search programs to scan millions of documents for suspect phrases and sentences.

Second, plagiarism cheats both the reader and the writer. At a fundamental level, citing a source is an academic courtesy. Because scholarship is an ongoing conversation, you should always presume that other students or scholars may want to use your work to develop their own. If you have taken an idea from another scholar but haven't cited it (or have cited it improperly), your reader will have no easy way of finding the source of the ideas that found their way into your work.

Perhaps the most serious problem raised when you plagiarize or fail to cite your sources is that you are cheating yourself. When you rely on the ideas of others to meet a course requirement, you are denying yourself the opportunity to have the best experience that college can offer: the opportunity to think for yourself. Writing papers can be difficult, and when deadlines loom it can be tempting to look for a shortcut—to lift ideas from scholars who clearly know more about the topic than you do. But it is *your* insight and opinion that your instructor wants to read. Consider each writing assignment as an opportunity to explore and express your ideas. Your education is no small expense; you might as well get your money's worth.

5

Developing Your Thesis

Writing a Thesis Sentence

No sentence in your paper will vex you as much as the thesis sentence—and with good reason: the thesis sentence is very often the one sentence in the paper that asserts, controls, and structures the entire argument. Without a strong, persuasive, thoughtful thesis—explicit or implied—a paper might seem weak, unfocused, and not worth the reader's time.

What makes a good thesis sentence? A good thesis sentence generally has the following characteristics:

A good thesis sentence makes a claim. This doesn't mean that you have to reduce an idea to an either-or proposition and then take a stand. Rather, you need to develop an interesting perspective that you can support and defend. This perspective must be more than a mere observation. "Learning to read and write is important for Frederick Douglass" is merely an observation. Douglass himself comments on that fact on several occasions in his *Narrative*. "Learning to read and write is the most important factor leading to Douglass's escape from slavery" is an argument. Why? Because this thesis posits a perspective. It makes a claim that engages competing claims. Put another way, a good thesis sentence inspires (rather than silences) other points of view. Someone else might argue that the incident in which Douglass fights Mr. Covey is the most important factor leading to Douglass's escape from slavery. Another might point to a third factor or a fourth. In short, if your thesis is positing something that no one can (or would bother to) argue with, then it is not a very good thesis.

A good thesis sentence determines the scope of the argument. The thesis sentence determines what you are required to say in a paper. It also determines what you cannot say. Every paragraph in your paper exists to support or elaborate on your thesis. Accordingly, if one paragraph you have written seems irrelevant to your thesis, then you have three choices: get rid of that paragraph, rewrite the thesis sentence, or work to make the paragraph more clearly relevant. Understand that you do not have a fourth option: you cannot simply include the idea without making clear its connection to your thesis. The thesis is like a contract between you and your reader. If you introduce ideas that the reader isn't prepared for or doesn't find relevant, then you've violated that contract.

A good thesis sentence provides a structure for the argument. The thesis sentence signals to the reader not only what your argument is but also how it will be presented. In other words, your thesis sentence should either directly or indirectly suggest the structure of your argument to the reader. Say, for example, that you are going to argue the following idea: "That learning to read and write is the most important factor leading to Douglass's escape from slavery is demonstrated in two incidents: A and B." In this case the reader understands that you are going to cover two important points, and that these points will appear in a certain order. If you suggest a particular organizing principle and then abandon it, the reader could feel irritated and confused.

Alternatives to the Thesis Sentence

Sometimes the purpose of a piece of writing is not to make a claim but to raise a series of questions. Other times a writer wants to leave a matter unresolved, inspiring readers to stake out their own positions. In these cases the thesis sentence might take other forms: the thesis question or the implied thesis.

As we have said, not every piece of writing sets out to make a claim. If your purpose as a writer is to explore, for instance, the reasons for the initial success of Amy Tan's *The Joy Luck Club* (a topic for which you are not yet prepared to make a claim), your *thesis question* might read, "What cultural forces conspired to make *The Joy Luck Club* a popular success?"

Note that this question, while provocative, does not offer a sense of the argument's structure. It permits the writer to pursue all ideas, without committing to any. Although this freedom might seem appealing, you will find that the lack of a declarative thesis statement actually requires more work. You will need to tighten your internal structure and paragraph-to-paragraph transitions so that the reader can easily follow your line of inquiry.

In pursuing the question "What cultural forces conspired to make *The Joy Luck Club* a popular success?," you might start by discussing the literary marketplace in the 1980s. What other books were selling well during this period? You might follow up by discussing the increasing popularity of ethnic American literature at the end of the decade. That discussion of ethnic literature might address concurrent debates about multiculturalism and the literary canon.

You can see that there is a lot of material to cover here—perhaps too much in a short paper. If you do not know where the paper will lead or what your conclusions will be, you might find it difficult to avoid digressing or following irrelevant tangents. Therefore, if you are going to use a thesis question rather than a thesis statement, be sure that it is a clearly articulated question—one that you can answer with a well-organized response. And if the paper starts to feel unwieldy, you might decide instead to use the thesis question as the beginning of a discovery draft. Your findings in the discovery draft can then lead to a more declarative thesis for the essay.

One of the most fascinating things about a thesis sentence is that it is the most important sentence in a paper, even when it's not there. In some essays you will find it difficult to point to a single sentence that declares the argument. Nonetheless, the essay is coherent and makes a point. In these cases the writers have used an implied thesis.

Writers use an implied thesis when they want readers to come to their own conclusions about the matter at hand. However, just because the writer doesn't explicitly declare the thesis doesn't mean that she or he is working without one. Good writers will always clearly state their thesis—even if it's only in their own mind or notes for the paper. They may elect not to put the thesis in the paper, but each paragraph, each sentence they write, is controlled by the thesis all the same.

If you decide to write a paper with an implied thesis, be sure that you have a strong grasp of your argument and its structure. Also be sure that you supply adequate transitions so that the reader can follow your argument with ease.

When you begin writing, you should have a solid, well-articulated thesis. The thesis will tell your readers the purpose of your essay, and it will help guide you as you write. However, keep in mind that your thesis is never set in stone; you can always modify it as needed. Often you will find that your thoughts about a topic evolve as you write; as a result, writers often revisit and refine their conclusions. But sometimes it will be necessary to change your thesis to reflect changes in your thinking. Therefore, when you begin writing, what you really have is a *working thesis*. It can change and adapt and develop as you write the paper. A working thesis doesn't become a final thesis until the paper is finished.

Turning Your Ideas into a Thesis

Now that you have a better sense for what makes for a successful thesis, let's consider how to create one based on work you've already completed. Let's say you've done some brainstorming and a little freewriting; maybe you've even written a discovery draft. You think you have some interesting and potentially original ideas, so, in the hopes of focusing those ideas, you nutshell. Now you just need to convert one of those focused ideas into a working thesis.

Composing a working thesis is challenging. After all, the thesis is your paper's most important sentence. It cannot be crafted formulaically but must reflect the complexities of the argument that you are hoping to write. But, formula or no, we can offer some advice to get you off on the right foot.

First you will want to determine what you want to write about. Since you have already generated some ideas through brainstorming, freewriting, and other exercises, you should have several options. You might choose a single observation from your list and focus on it, or you might look for an idea that ties together two or three of these observations, and focus on that. Whatever you decide, don't try to squeeze everything you have observed into a single essay. To do so would require a book—and you simply don't have time to write a book before the paper is due. Determining which idea or set of ideas you want to work with will enable you to stay focused; it will also let you do justice to your ideas in the limited time that you have.

Sometimes writers are torn between two or three very good observations. If the ideas cannot be synthesized into a single idea or claim, the best strategy is to pick whichever observation looks most interesting or unusual or compelling. In other words, choose the observation that you can have the most fun with. Doing so will help you stay focused: you now know not only what you want to discuss but also what you can leave alone.

At this point in the process you might notice something odd: even though you don't have a thesis yet, the observation you have chosen to write about will help to dictate which type of paper you will write. If your observation has to do with the way a regional writer highlights linguistic differ-ence (for example, Sarah Orne Jewett's use of dialect in "The Foreigner"), then you will most likely be writing a textual analysis paper. Realizing this helps you understand not only what you are going to do but also what you are not going to do: a paper about context, comparison, or adapta-tion, for example.

So now you have your plan: you're going to write a textual analysis paper about dialect in Jewett's "The Foreigner." As we noted earlier in this guide, your goal in writing a textual analysis paper is to choose a small textual element and examine in detail how that element contributes to the major themes, underlying message, or overall effect of the text. At this point you need to compose a question, using this goal to guide you. After some doodling you come up with this question: How does Jewett's use of dialect contribute to the theme of foreignness in the story? Give yourself the opportunity to explore that question. Brainstorm or freewrite a response. Then try to shape your response so that you can answer the question in a couple of sentences. Then try to do it in a single sentence. When you can answer that question in one sentence, you will have your working thesis.

Of course, if you were writing a contextual analysis paper, you would ask yourself a different question, based on the goals of that type of paper. The same is true for an adaptation paper. The strategy is clear: instead of trying to create a thesis out of thin air, pick an element of the literary work that interests you, then ask yourself a relevant question based on the goals of the type of paper you are going to write. When you answer your own question, you will have a working thesis.

The Thesis Sentence Checklist

In the end you may have spent a good deal of time writing your working thesis and still not know if it is a good one. As we have indicated earlier, a good thesis typically evolves as the writer writes. You will want to interrogate your thesis throughout the writing process to determine how well it is holding up. Here are some questions to ask yourself as you write:

Does the thesis sentence attempt to answer or to explore a challenging intellectual question? If your thesis doesn't challenge you, it likely won't challenge your reader either. If you find yourself bored as you write, or if you are haunted by the sense that you aren't talking about anything important, stop writing. Return to your list of observations. See if you can find some connection between the observations that might raise the intellectual stakes of your paper.

Will the point I'm making generate discussion and argument, or will it leave people asking "So what?"? If your thesis doesn't generate discussion, perhaps the point you made is too obvious or insignificant. Return to your list of observations. Ask of each one, "Why is this important?" The answer to that question should help you refine your thesis.

Is the thesis too vague? Or too general? Should you focus on a more specific aspect of the topic? If a thesis is too broad, it's unlikely to hold the reader's interest. Take your more general idea and link it to specific observations about the text. Perhaps in that linkage you will find the focus for your paper.

Does the thesis deal directly with the topic at hand, or is it a declaration of my personal feelings? Be careful about personal opinions: making a claim is different from declaring an opinion. An academic paper does the former but avoids the latter.

Does the thesis indicate the direction of my argument? Does it suggest a structure for my paper? If a thesis is well constructed, it will suggest to you and your reader where the paper is headed. Look at your thesis. Then look at your outline. Does your thesis reflect or suggest that outline? Can you rewrite the thesis so that the outline (or structure) is suggested?

Does the introductory paragraph define terms important to my thesis? Don't make your thesis do all the work. Rely on your introduction to help your thesis along, especially when it comes to necessary but cumbersome tasks, such as defining terms.

If I am writing a research paper, does the introduction place my thesis within the larger, ongoing scholarly dis-

cussion about the topic? Consider again the dinner party metaphor. What do the scholars at the table have to say about the topic? What do you have to say in response to their ideas? Is the relationship between your perspective and theirs clear to the reader? If not, how might it be made clear?

6

Considering Structure and Organization

Once you have figured out what you want to say, you are left with the problem of how to say it. How should you begin the paper? Should you address the opinions of other thinkers? And what should you do with that stubborn contradiction you've uncovered in your own thinking?

Writing papers in college requires you to come up with sophisticated, complex, and even creative ways of structuring your ideas. Accordingly, we cannot—and will not—offer simple formulas that will work for every paper, every time. We can, however, give you some prompts that will help you to consider the structure of your paper.

Let Your Thesis Direct You

Begin by listening to your thesis. If it is well written, it will tell you which direction to go with your paper. Suppose, for example, that in responding to Ralph Waldo Emerson's essay "Experience," you have written a thesis that says:

> While it claims to be a broad philosophical meditation on human experience, Emerson's essay—a quiet lament for the death of his son, Waldo—is in fact a treatise on the importance of loss and grief in human development.

This thesis provides you with several clues about how best to structure the paper, and it prepares readers for what they will encounter therein. For instance, your thesis promises readers that the paper will argue for the importance of a spectral presence in the essay. Emerson notes, "Grief too will make us idealists. In the death of my son, now more than two years ago, I seem to have lost a beautiful estate,—no more. I cannot get it nearer to me." The paper will likely begin by acknowledging that, although this is a single reference in a very long essay, Emerson's grief for his son is everywhere in "Experience." The rest of the paper will then show how central loss and grief are to Emerson's ideas about human experience.

We say that loss and grief are central to Emerson's ideas about human experience not necessarily because Emerson himself said so but because you seem to say so in your thesis. Reread the thesis sentence. Note that the emphasis falls on its second half: "Emerson's essay . . . is in fact a treatise on the importance of loss and grief in human development." We know that this clause is the emphatic clause because it is grammatically independent. In other words, it can stand alone. The independent clause also includes the phrase "in fact," which suggests the purported truth of what follows. Such an emphasis tells us that we will be given not simply an analysis of Emerson's essay, but, rather, an analysis of how loss, grief, and Emerson's own biography help to structure "Experience." We understand all of this because you took the time to write an emphatic thesis.

Sketching Your Argument

Although your thesis will identify your paper's general direction, it will not necessarily provide you with a plan for how to organize all of your points, both large and small. In this instance it might be helpful to diagram or sketch your argument.

In sketching your argument, the goal is to fill the page with your ideas. Begin by writing your thesis. Put it where your instincts tell you to: at the top of the page, in the center, at the bottom. Around the thesis, cluster the points you want to make. Under each of these points, note the observations you have made and the evidence you will use. Don't worry if your sketch starts to look messy. Use arrows. Draw circles. Take up colored pens. Any of these methods can help you find connections between your ideas that might otherwise go unnoticed. Working from your sketch, try to see the line of reasoning that is emerging from the mess.

Sketching is an important step in the writing process because it allows you to explore visually the connections between your ideas. If you outline a paper too early in the process, you risk missing these connections. That is, you risk lining up your points—A, B, C—without fully understanding why you are doing so. Sketching your argument helps you see, for example, that points A and C really overlap and need to be thought through more carefully.

Outlining Your Argument

When you have finished the sketch, you are ready to make an outline. The task of the outline is to identify the paper's best structure. By "best structure" we mean the structure that best supports the argument you intend to make.

When you are outlining a paper, you have many options for organization. Understand, however, that each choice you make eliminates dozens of other options. Your goal is to come up with an outline in which all your choices support your thesis.

Treat the outline as if it were a puzzle you are putting together. In a puzzle, each piece has only one appropriate place. The same should be true of your paper. If it is easy to shift around your ideas—if several of your paragraphs could be switched around and no one would be the wiser—then you haven't yet found the best structure for your paper. Each paragraph should present a single, well-supported idea that is the logical successor to the ideas that preceded it, all of them building inexorably toward your paper's overall point—the thesis. Keep working until your outline fits your ideas like a glove.

When you think you have an outline that works, challenge it, as if it were a source from your research. The first outline rarely holds up to a good interrogation. When you start asking questions of your outline, you will begin to see where the plan holds and where it falls apart. Here are some questions you might ask:

Does my thesis control the direction of the outline?

Are all of my main points relevant to the thesis?

Can any of these points be moved around without changing something important about the thesis?

Does the outline seem logical?

Does the argument progress, or does it stall out anywhere?

If the argument seems to take a sudden turn, does the thesis anticipate that turn?

Do I have sufficient support for each of my points?

Have I made room in the outline for other points of view about the topic?

Does this outline reflect a thorough, thoughtful argument?

Constructing Paragraphs

Imagine that you have written the thesis and interrogated the outline. You know which modes of arrangement you intend to use, and you have settled on a plan that you think will work. Now you have to go about the serious business of constructing paragraphs.

You were probably told in high school that paragraphs are the workhorses of a paper. Indeed they are. If a single paragraph is incoherent or weak, the entire argument might fail. It is important that you consider carefully the "job" of each paragraph. Know what you want that paragraph to do. Extending the metaphor, make sure it pulls its weight.

WHAT IS A PARAGRAPH?

A paragraph is generally understood as a single "unit" of a paper. When readers encounter a new paragraph, they expect that you are going to declare a point and then offer support for that point. If you violate this expectation—if your paragraphs wander aimlessly among a half dozen points, or if they declare points without offering any evidence to support them—readers will become confused or irritated by your argument. Put simply, they won't want to read any further.

WHAT SHOULD A PARAGRAPH DO?

A good paragraph is not unlike a good friend. You want a friend who is supportive, strong, and considerate. Similarly, a good paragraph is:

- **Supportive.** Even in the most trying of times a good paragraph finds a way to support the thesis. Its relationship to the thesis is clear.

- **Strong.** A good paragraph is well formed. It's neither bloated nor underdeveloped. It develops its main idea, using strong and sufficient evidence.

- **Considerate.** A good paragraph considers its relationship to other paragraphs. It never interrupts its fellow paragraphs to babble on about its own irrelevant problems. It waits its turn. It shows up when and where it is supposed to. It doesn't make a mess for other paragraphs to clean up. In other words, a considerate paragraph is a coherent paragraph. It makes sense within the text as a whole.

WRITING THE TOPIC SENTENCE OR GUIDING CLAIM

Just as every paper requires a thesis sentence to assert and control its argument, so also every paragraph requires a topic sentence to assert and control its main idea. Without a topic sentence, your paragraphs will seem jumbled and aimless, and your reader will become confused. Because the topic sentence plays an important role in your paragraph, it must be crafted with care. When you have written a topic sentence, ask yourself the following questions:

Does the topic sentence declare a single point of the argument? Because the reader expects that a paragraph will explore only one idea, it is important that your topic sentence not be too ambitious. If it points to two or three ideas, perhaps you need to consider developing more paragraphs.

Does the topic sentence further the argument? Give your topic sentences the same "so what?" test that you gave your thesis sentence. If your topic sentence isn't interesting, your paragraph probably won't further the argument. As a result, your paper could stall.

Is the topic sentence relevant to the thesis? It might seem so to you, but the relevance may not be clear to your reader. If you find that your topic sentence is taking you into new territory, stop writing and consider your options. If the new territory isn't relevant to the existing thesis, either you will have to rewrite your thesis to accommodate this new direction or you will have to consider excluding this paragraph from your final paper. (Such exclusions are a frustrating but quite common experience: all academic writers produce more ideas than they can possibly use in a single paper.)

Is there a clear relationship between this topic sentence and the paragraph that came before it? Make sure that you haven't left out any steps in the process of composing your argument. If you take a sudden turn in your reasoning, signal that turn to the reader by using the proper transitional phrase—"on the other hand," "however," or the like.

Does the topic sentence control the paragraph? If your paragraph seems to unravel, perhaps the topic sentence isn't adequately controlling the paragraph and needs to be rewritten. Or maybe the paragraph is moving on to a new idea that needs to be developed in a paragraph of its own.

Where have I placed my topic sentence? Readers often look for topic sentences at or near the beginning of a paragraph. Consider this: If you are skimming something quickly, which sentence do you look to in each paragraph? Likely it is the first sentence. But that doesn't mean all of your topic sentences need to be situated at the beginning of your paragraphs. If you are going to place your topic sentence elsewhere, however, you will need to craft your paragraph with care. You might justify putting the topic sentence in the middle of the paragraph, for example, if you have information that needs to precede it. You might also justify putting the topic sentence at the end of the paragraph if you want the reader to consider your line of reasoning before you declare your main point. Let the needs of your argument dictate where you place your topic sentence. And wherever you place it, be strategic: make sure that your decision facilitates your argument.

Developing Your Paragraphs

EVIDENCE

Students often ask how long a paragraph should be. To this we respond, "As long as it takes."

It is indeed possible to make a point quickly. And sometimes it is desirable to keep a paragraph short and sweet. Notice the preceding paragraph, for example. We might have hemmed and hawed, talked about short paragraphs and long paragraphs. We might have said that the average paragraph is one-half to two-thirds of a page in length. We might have spent time explaining why the too-short paragraph is too short and the too-long paragraph too long. Instead, we cut to the chase. After huffing and puffing through this paragraph (which is getting longer and longer all the time), we will give you the same advice: a good paragraph is as long as it needs to be in order to illustrate, explore, and/or prove its main idea.

However, length isn't all that matters in paragraph development. What is important is that a paragraph develops its idea fully and in a manner that readers can follow with ease.

Let's consider these two issues carefully. First, how do we know when an idea is fully developed? If your topic sentence is well written, it should tell you what the paragraph needs to do. If the topic sentence declares, for example, that there are two conflicting impulses at work in a particular fictional character, then the reader will expect the two impulses to be defined and illustrated. It might take two paragraphs to do this; it might take one. The decision will depend on how important this matter is to the discussion. If the point is important, then you will take your time, and (more likely than not) use at least two paragraphs. In this case a topic sentence might be understood as controlling not only a paragraph but an entire section of the paper.

When you have written a paragraph, ask yourself the following questions:

Do I have enough evidence to support this paragraph's idea?

Do I have too much evidence?

Does this evidence clearly support the assertion that I'm making in this paragraph, or am I stretching it?

If I'm stretching it, what can I do to convince the reader that this stretch is worth making?

Am I repeating myself in this paragraph?

Have I defined all of the paragraph's important terms?

Can I say, in a nutshell, what the purpose of this paragraph is?

Has the paragraph fulfilled that purpose?

ARRANGEMENT

Equally important to the idea of a paragraph's development is the paragraph's arrangement. Paragraphs are arranged differently for different purposes. For example, if you are writing a paper about a novel and wish to summarize a sequence of events, you will likely want to arrange the information chronologically. If you are writing a paper in which you want to describe the growing popularity of a particular genre, perhaps you will choose to arrange the information spatially. And if you are writing a paper about the elements of a poem that make it stand out from other poems of a similar type, you might want to arrange your ideas by working from the specific to the general—and so on.

COHERENCE

So you have your thesis, your topic sentences, and truckloads of evidence to support the whole lot. You have spent three days writing your paragraphs, making sure that each argues one point and that this point is well supported with textual evidence. But when you read the essay back to yourself, you feel a profound sense of disappointment. Although you have followed your outline, the essay just doesn't seem to hold together. It could be that you have a problem with coherence.

A lack of coherence is easy to diagnose but not so easy to cure. An incoherent essay just doesn't seem to flow. Its arguments are hard to understand and disjointed. The reader has to double back again and again in order to pick up the thread of the argument. Something has gone wrong, but what?

Look for the following issues in your paper:

Make sure the grammatical subjects of your sentences reflect the real subject of your paragraph. Underline the subjects of all the sentences in the paragraph. Do these subjects match the paragraph's subject in most cases? Or have you put the paragraph's subject into another, less important part of the sentence? Remember that the reader understands an idea's importance according to where you place it. If your main idea is hidden as an object of a preposition in a subordinate clause, your reader is going to struggle mightily to follow what you are saying. For instance, consider the following paragraph about the way Frederick Douglass discusses religion in *Narrative of the Life of Frederick Douglass*. The grammatical subject of each sentence is underlined.

Many <u>situations</u> occur throughout Douglass's *Narrative* in which Douglass witnesses slaveholders using the Bible to justify their actions. An excellent <u>example</u> is Master Thomas's conversion. Beforehand, <u>Thomas</u> had "relied upon his own depravity to shield and sustain him in his savage barbarity, but after his conversion, he found religious sanction and support for his slaveholding cruelty." This <u>idea</u> appears most clearly when he whips a woman while quoting scripture: "He that knoweth his master's will, and doeth it not, shall be beaten with many stripes."

Look at the four subjects: "situations," "example," "Thomas," and "idea." Of these, only "Thomas" is clearly related to the topic of the paragraph. Now consider this revised paragraph:

> Throughout his *Narrative*, <u>Douglass</u> offers several instances of slaveholders who use the Bible to justify their actions. <u>He</u> recounts in particular the story of Master Thomas, who "relied upon his own depravity to shield and sustain him in his savage barbarity, but who, after his conversion . . . found religious sanction and support for his slaveholding cruelty." <u>Douglass</u> elaborates by relating an incident in which Master Thomas, while whipping a naked woman with a heavy cow skin, justifies his actions by quoting scripture: "He that knoweth his master's will, and doeth it not, shall be beaten with many stripes."

Look at the subjects here: all three refer to Douglass. The paragraph's string of related subjects keeps the reader focused on the topic and creates a paragraph that flows more naturally and seems much more coherent than the first one.

Make sure the grammatical subjects are consistent. Again, look at the grammatical subjects of all your sentences. How many different subjects do you find? If you have too many different sentence subjects, your paragraph will be hard to follow.

Make sure your sentences look backward as well as forward. For a paragraph to be coherent, each sentence should begin by linking itself firmly to the sentence that preceded it. If the link between sentences does not seem firm, use an introductory clause or phrase to connect one idea to the other.

Follow the principle of moving from old to new. If you put the old information at the beginning of the sentence and the new information at the end, you accomplish two things. First, you ensure that your readers are on solid ground, moving from the familiar to the unknown. Second, you ensure that, because we tend to give emphasis to what comes at the end of a sentence, readers rightfully perceive that the new information is more important than the old.

Use repetition to create a sense of unity. Repeating key words and phrases at appropriate moments will give your readers a sense of coherence in your work. But don't overdo it; repetition can quickly become redundancy.

Use transition markers wisely. Sometimes you will need to announce to your readers a turn in your argument, or you will want to emphasize a point, or you will try to make clear a particular relationship in time. In all these cases you will want to use transition markers. Some examples follow:

- **To give an example:** *for example, for instance*
- **To present a list:** *first, second, third, next, then*

- **To show that you have more to say:** *in addition, furthermore, moreover*
- **To indicate similarity:** *also, likewise, similarly*
- **To show an exception:** *but, however, nevertheless, on the other hand*
- **To show cause and effect:** *accordingly, consequently, therefore, because*
- **To emphasize:** *indeed, in fact, of course*
- **To conclude:** *finally, in conclusion, in the end*

Introductions and Conclusions

Introductions and conclusions are among the most challenging of all paragraphs. Why? Because they do much more than state a topic sentence and offer support. Introductions and conclusions must synthesize and provide context for your entire argument; moreover, they must also make the proper impression on your readers.

The introduction is your chance to get readers interested in your subject. Accordingly, the tone of the paragraph has to be just right. You want to inform, but not to the point of being dull; you want to intrigue, but not to the point of being vague; you want to take a strong stance, but not to the point of being obnoxious. Pay attention to the nuances of your tone. Seek out a second reader if you are not sure that you've managed to get the tone the way you want it.

Equally important to the tone of the introduction is that it needs to place your argument in a larger context. Here are strategies for doing so:

Announce your topic broadly; then declare your particular take. For example, if you are interested in talking about the symbolism in Stephen Crane's "The Open Boat," you might (1) begin by saying that Crane's symbolism has posed a problem for many of his critics, (2) provide a quick definition of the problem as others have defined it, and (3) declare your thesis (which states your own position on the matter).

Provide any background material important to your argument. If you are interested in exploring how writers of the modernist movement influenced the work of Robert Pinsky, in your introduction you will want to provide, in broad strokes, a description of modernism. Don't include irrelevant details in your description; instead, emphasize those aspects of the movement that might have most influenced Pinsky.

Define key terms as you intend to make use of them in your argument. If, for example, you're writing a paper on Elizabeth Bishop's use of the villanelle, then it is absolutely essential that you define the term for your reader. Begin with a definition of terms, and from there work toward the declaration of your argument.

Use an anecdote or a quotation. Sometimes you will find a terrific story or quotation that seems to reflect the main point of your paper. Don't be afraid to begin with it. Be sure, however, that you tie that story or quotation clearly and immediately to your main argument.

Acknowledge your opponents. When you are writing a paper about a controversial matter, you might wish to begin by summarizing the point of view of your opponents. Then state your own position in opposition to theirs. In this way you place yourself clearly in the ongoing conversation.

Remember, the introduction is the first impression that your argument will make on the reader. Take special care with your sentences so that they will be cogent and compelling. Also take the time to consider who your readers are and what they will bring with them to their reading. If your readers are very knowledgeable about the subject, you will not need to provide a lot of background information. If your readers are less knowledgeable, you will need to be more careful about defining terms.

Finally, you might want to consider writing the introduction after you have written the rest of the paper. Many writers find that they have a better grip on their subject once they have done a first draft. This "better grip" helps them craft an introduction that is sure-footed, persuasive, interesting, and clear. But be careful: any changes you make to an introduction and/or a thesis statement will affect the paper that follows. Simply adding the new introductory paragraph will not magically produce a "completed" paper.

Conclusions are also difficult to write. How do you manage to make the reader feel persuaded by what you have said? Even if the points of your paper are strong, the overall effect of your argument might fall to pieces if the paper as a whole is badly concluded.

Many students end their papers by simply summarizing what has come before. A summary of what the reader has just read is important to the conclusion—particularly if your argument has been complicated or has covered a lot of ground. But a good conclusion will do more. If the introduction sought to place the paper in the larger, ongoing conversation about the topic, the conclusion should return readers to that ongoing conversation—but now having learned something new about the topic. Again, you never want a reader to finish your paper and say "So what?"

Many of the strategies for improving introductions can help to improve your conclusions as well. In the conclusion you might do the following:

Return to the ongoing conversation, emphasizing the importance of your own contribution to it.

Consider again the background information with which you began, and illustrate how your argument has shed new light on that information.

Return to your key terms and point out how your essay has added a new dimension to their meanings.

Use an anecdote or a quotation that summarizes or reflects your main idea.

Acknowledge your opponents—if only to emphasize that you have successfully countered their positions.

Remember, word choice is especially important to a conclusion. Your goal in the final sentences is to leave your ideas resounding in the reader's mind. Give the reader something to think about, and make your language ring.

7

Attending to Style

Most of us know good style when we see it—and, especially, when we *hear* it in the mind's ear. We also know when a sentence seems cumbersome or convoluted. However, although we can easily spot beastly sentences, it is not as easy to say why a sentence—especially one that is grammatically correct—isn't working. We look at the sentence; we see that the commas are in the right places; we find no glaring error. So why is the sentence so awful? What has gone wrong?

When thinking about what makes a good sentence, be sure to put yourself in the reader's place. What is a reader hoping to find in your sentences? Information, yes. Eloquence, surely. But, most important, a reader is looking for clarity. Your reader does not want to wrestle with sentences. She wants to read with ease. She wants to see one idea build on another. She wants to experience the force of your language and the importance of your idea. Above all, she wants to feel that you, the writer, are doing the bulk of the work. Put simply, she wants to read sentences that are persuasive, straightforward, and clear. (This approach to style has been greatly influenced by Joseph Williams. His *Style: Lessons in Clarity and Grace*, 11th ed. [New York: Pearson Longman, 2013] is highly recommended.)

Basic Principles of the Sentence

FOCUS ON ACTORS AND ACTIONS

To understand what makes a good sentence, it is important to understand one principle: a sentence, at its very basic level, is about actors and actions. As such, the subject of a sentence should point clearly to the actor, and the verb of the sentence should describe the important action.

This principle might seem so obvious that you think it doesn't warrant further discussion. But think again. Look at the following sentence, and then try to determine what's wrong with it:

> There is a question in the mind of some critics over whether the employment of extensive dialogue is a sign of weakness in a novel.

This sentence has no grammatical errors. But certainly it lumbers along, without any force. What are the actors? What are the actions?

Now consider the following sentence:

Some critics question whether extensive dialogue signifies a weak novel.

What happened to this sentence? We can point to the most obvious changes: the empty *there is* phrase is omitted; the abstract noun *sign* is replaced with the stronger verb *signify*; a second abstract noun, *weakness,* is replaced with the adjective *weak*; all of the prepositions that the abstract nouns require are omitted. What principle governs these many changes? Precisely the one mentioned earlier: that the *actors* in a sentence should serve as the sentence's grammatical subjects, and the *actions* should be illustrated forcefully in the sentence's verbs.

Whenever you feel that your prose is confusing or hard to follow, find the actors and the actions of your sentences. Is the actor the subject of your sentence? Is the action related, vividly, in a verb? If not, then rewrite your sentences accordingly.

BE CONCRETE

Student writers tend to rely too heavily on abstract nouns: they use *expectation* when the verb *expect* is stronger; they write *evaluation* when *evaluate* is more vivid. So why use an abstract noun when a verb will do better? Many students believe that abstract nouns permit them to sound more "academic." When you write with a lot of abstract nouns, however, you risk confusing your reader. You also end up cornering yourself syntactically. Consider the following:

Nouns often require prepositions. Too many prepositional phrases in a sentence are hard to follow. Verbs, on the other hand, can stand on their own. They are cleaner; they don't box you in. If you need some proof of this claim, consider the following sentence:

> An evaluation of the revised script by the director is necessary prior to our blocking out process.

Notice all of the prepositional phrases these nouns require. Now look at the following sentence, which uses verbs:

> The director must evaluate the revised script before we block it.

This sentence has fewer nouns and prepositions and is therefore much easier to read—yet it still conveys all the information found in the prior sentence.

Abstract nouns often invite the *there is* construction. Consider the following sentence:

> There is a method of narration that Zora Neale Hurston used called "free indirect discourse" in which the charac-

teristics of third-person speech are combined with the characteristics of first-person speech.

We might rewrite this sentence as follows:

> Zora Neale Hurston used a method of narration called "free indirect discourse" that combines characteristics of first- and third-person speech.

The result, again, is a sentence that is more direct and easier to read.

Abstract nouns are, well, abstract. Using too many abstract nouns will make your prose seem ungrounded. Words such as *falsification*, *beauteousness*, and *insubstantiality* sound pompous and vague—which may be exactly what you want if you're striving for a slightly comic, self-mocking effect. But, by and large, people simply don't talk this way. Instead, you should use concrete nouns (and strong verbs) to convey your ideas. *Lying*, *beauty*, and *flimsiness* reflect the way people really speak; these words point directly to their meanings without drawing undue attention to themselves.

Abstract nouns can obscure your logic. Note how hard it is to follow the line of reasoning in the following sentence (the nouns that might be rewritten as verbs or as adjectives are in boldface):

> **Decisions** with regard to **the elimination** of characters from a novel on the basis of **their insignificance** to the developing narrative rest with the author.

Now consider this sentence:

> When characters are no longer significant to a narrative, the author can decide to eliminate them from his novel.

The exception: When to use abstract nouns.

In some instances an abstract noun will be essential to the sentence. Sometimes abstract nouns refer to a previous sentence (e.g., *these arguments, this decision*). Other times an abstract noun will allow you to be more concise (e.g., *her argument* versus *what she argued*). And, occasionally, an abstract noun is a concept important to your argument: freedom, love, revolution, and so on. Still, if you examine your prose, you will probably find that you overuse abstract nouns. Omitting all unnecessary abstract nouns will make for leaner, "fitter" prose.

BE CONCISE

Most students do not know how to write concisely. Students tend to use phrases when a single word will do; offer pairs of adjectives and verbs where one is enough; or overwrite, saying the same thing two or three times.

Fortunately, concision is just a few edits away. It is easy to delete words and phrases from your prose once you have learned to be ruthless about it. Ask yourself: Do I really need words like *actually, basically, generally,* and so on? Am I using two words where one will do? Isn't the phrase *first and foremost* redundant? What's the point of *future* in *future plans*? And why do I keep saying, *"In my opinion"?* Doesn't the reader understand that this is my paper, based on my point of view? Does drawing attention to myself in this way make my points any stronger—or does it have the opposite effect, coming across as insecurity or as hedging?

Sometimes you won't be able to fix a wordy sentence by simply deleting a few words or phrases. Instead, you will have to rewrite the entire sentence. Take the following sentence, for example:

> Plagiarism is a serious academic offense resulting in punishments that might include suspension or dismissal, profoundly affecting your academic career.

The idea here is simple: *Plagiarism is a serious offense with serious consequences.* Why not simply say so? Don't be afraid to let your reader connect your ideas to the context. At its most pleasurable, good writing gives the reader a sense of collaboration, of being trusted to connect the dots.

BE COHERENT

We will now move from the sentence as a discrete unit to the way that sentences fit together. Coherence (or the lack of it) is a common problem in student papers. Sometimes an instructor encounters a paper in which all the ideas seem to be there but are hard to follow nonetheless. The prose seems jumbled. The line of reasoning is anything but linear. Couldn't the student have made this paper a bit more readable, the exhausted instructor laments?

Although coherence is a complicated and difficult matter to address, we can offer a couple of tricks that will help your sentences "flow." The first trick draws on American wedding culture, of all things. Like the bride, your sentences should wear "something old and something new." Most of your sentences should begin by looking back to the previous sentence (something old). Then the sentence should give the reader any new or additional information (something new). If you outfit your sentences accordingly, your line of reasoning will be much easier to follow. Though this advice sounds simple enough, it is not always easy to follow. Let's dissect the practice so that we can better understand how our sentences might be "well dressed."

Consider, first, the beginnings of sentences. The coherence of your paper depends largely on how well you begin sentences. "Well begun is half done," says Mary Poppins, and in this case (as in all cases, really) she is right.

Beginning a sentence is hard work. When you begin a sentence, you have three important matters to consider:

1. **Is your topic also the subject of the sentence?** When a sentence lacks coherence, usually it is because the writer

has not been careful to ensure that the topic of the sentence is also the grammatical subject of the sentence. If, for instance, you're writing a paper about Lucille Clifton, and at one point you include a sentence whose topic is the importance of lowercase typography in her poetry, then the grammatical subject of the sentence should reflect that idea:

> **Clifton's lowercase letters** are a crucial element of her poetry since they suggest both informality and a breaking from poetic convention.

If, on the other hand, you bury your topic in a subordinate clause, look what happens:

> An important part of Clifton's poetry is the typography, such as **her lowercase letters,** which suggest both informality and a breaking from poetic convention.

The emphasis and focus of the sentence are obscured.

2. **Are the topics/subjects of your sentences consistent?** For a paragraph to be coherent, most of the sentence subjects should be the same. To check for consistency, pick out a paragraph and make a list of its sentence subjects. See if any of the subjects seem out of place. For example, suppose you're writing a paragraph comparing the experience of time in the narratives of Olaudah Equiano and Harriet Jacobs. Do most of your grammatical subjects reflect that

paragraph topic? Or do some of your sentences have other, tangential topics as the grammatical subject? You will confuse readers if your paragraph's sentence subjects point to too many competing ideas. Revise the sentences (and perhaps the entire paragraph) for coherence.

3. **Have you marked, when appropriate, the transitions between ideas?** As we've said, coherence depends on how well you connect a sentence to the one that came before it. You will want to make elegant transitions between your sentences, using words such as *however* or *therefore* when necessary. You will also want to signal to readers whenever something important or disappointing comes up. In these cases you will want to use expressions such as *note that* or *unfortunately*. You might also want to indicate time or place in your argument. If so, use transitions such as *then, later, earlier*, or *in the previous paragraph*.

But a word to the wise: be careful not to overuse transitional phrases. Some writers think transitional phrases can, all by themselves, direct a reader through an argument. Indeed, sometimes all a paragraph needs is a *however* in order for its argument to suddenly make sense. More often, though, a problem of coherence stems from the writer not articulating for himself the connections between his ideas. So don't rely on transitional phrases alone to give sense to muddled prose.

BE EMPHATIC

We have been talking about how sentences begin, but what about how they end?

If the beginnings of sentences must look over their shoulders at what came before, the ends of sentences must forge ahead into new ground. It is the end of a sentence, then, that must be courageous and emphatic. You must construct sentences so that the ends pack a punch.

To write emphatically, follow these principles:

Declare important ideas at the end of a sentence. Shift less important ideas to the front.

Tighten the ends of sentences. Don't trail off into nonsense, don't repeat yourself, and don't qualify what you've just said if you don't have to. Simply make your point and move on.

Use subordinate clauses to house subordinate ideas. Put all the important ideas in main clauses and the less important ideas in subordinate clauses. If you have two ideas of equal importance that you want to express in the same sentence, then use parallel constructions or semicolons. These two tricks of the trade are perhaps more useful than any others in balancing equally significant ideas.

BE IN CONTROL

When sentences run on and on, readers know that a writer has lost control. Take command of your sentences. When you read over your paper, look for sentences that never seem to end. (You might even count the number of printed lines in each sentence. Sentences that require more than three printed lines are often wordy or convoluted or both.) Your first impulse might be to take these long sentences and divide them into two (or three or four) smaller sentences. This simple solution sometimes works. But often this strategy isn't the most desirable one; it might lead to short, choppy sentences. Moreover, if you always cut your sentences in two, then you will never learn how a sentence can be long and complex and still be good prose.

What do you do when you encounter an overly long sentence? First consider the point of your sentence. Usually it will have more than one point, and sorting out the points will help to sort out the grammar. Consider carefully the points you are trying to make as well as the connections between those points. Then try to determine which grammatical structure best serves your purpose.

Are the points of equal importance? Use a coordinating conjunction (e.g., *and, but, or*) or a semicolon to join the ideas. Try to use parallel constructions when appropriate.

Are the points of unequal importance? Use subordinate clauses (e.g., *although, while, because,* and so on) or relative clauses (e.g., *that, which*) to join the ideas, putting the less important idea in the subordinate position.

Does one point make for an interesting aside? Insert that point between commas, dashes, or even parentheses at the appropriate juncture in the sentence.

Do these ideas belong in the same sentence? If not, create two sentences.

WRITE BEAUTIFULLY

In your career as a writer you will sometimes produce a paper that is well written but could be written better. On this happy occasion, you might wish to turn your attention to such matters as balance, parallel structure, emphasis, rhythm, and word choice. If you are interested in exploring these rhetorical tools, consult one of several excellent style books, such as Joseph Williams's *Style: Lessons in Clarity and Grace*, William Strunk Jr. and E. B. White's *The Elements of Style*, or John Trimble's *Writing with Style*. You will find plenty of valuable advice in any one of these sources.

Karen Gocsik and
Coleman Hutchison,
<u>Writing About
American Literature</u>

(New York: W.W. Norton
& Co., 2014)

8

Revising Your Work

Why and How to Revise

Most of us who compose on a computer understand revision as an ongoing—even constant—process. Every time you hit the delete key, every time you cut and paste, and every time you take out a comma or exchange one word for another, you are revising.

Real revision, however, is more than making a few changes here and there. As the word implies, revision calls for *seeing again;* it requires that you open yourself up to the possibility that parts of your paper—even your entire paper—might need to be rethought and rewritten.

Achieving this state of mind is difficult. First, you might be very attached to what you've written. You might be unwilling to change a word, let alone three or four paragraphs. Second, there is the question of time: you might sense that the paper needs major work, but it is due tomorrow, or you have an exam in physics, or you are coming down with a cold and know that you need to sleep. Third, you might have difficulty understanding what, exactly, is wrong with your paper. Finally, you might simply be sick and tired of the paper. How can you make another pass through it when exhaustion has you in its grip? Why should you be bothered with the process of revising?

Perhaps we can convince you that revision is worth the extra effort simply by saying that revising a paper will help you achieve a better grade. A good reader can sense when a piece of writing has been thoroughly considered and reconsidered. This consideration (and here we use the word in both of its meanings) is not lost on your instructor and will be rewarded.

More important than grades, however, is the fact that revising teaches you to be a better writer. Professional writers know that to write is to rewrite. In the revision process you improve both your reading skills and your analytical skills. You learn to challenge your own ideas, thus deepening and strengthening your argument. You also learn to find the weaknesses in your writing. You may even discover patterns of error or habits of organization that are undermining your papers.

Though revising takes time and effort, it will help you to become a more efficient writer down the road. If, for example, you have discovered through the revision process that you tend to bury your topic sentences in the middle of your paragraphs, then you can take this discovery with you as you draft

your next paper. You may then be less likely to make that particular mistake again.

Perhaps we have answered the question "Why should I
revise?" The next question is "How?" There are many different kinds of revising, including the following:

Large-scale revision. Large-scale revision means looking at
the entire paper for places where your thinking seems to go
awry. You might need to provide evidence, define terms, or
add an entirely new step to your reasoning. You might even
decide to restructure or rewrite your paper completely if you
discover a new idea that intrigues you or a structure that seems
to be more effective than the one you have been using.

Small-scale revision. Small-scale revision needs to happen
when you know that a certain part of your paper just isn't
working. Maybe the introduction needs work. Maybe one part
of the argument seems weak. Once you have located the problem, you can focus on revising that one section of your paper.
When you are finished you will want to reconsider your
paper as a whole to make sure that your revisions work in the
context of the entire paper.

Editing. Too often students confuse editing with revision.
They are not the same. Editing is the process of finding minor
problems with a text—problems that might easily be fixed by
deleting a word or sentence, cutting and pasting a paragraph,
and so on. When you edit, you are considering your reader.

You might be happy with how you have written your paper, but will your reader find it clear, readable, and interesting? How can you rewrite the paper so that it is clearer, more concise, and, most important of all, a pleasure to read?

The very best writers revise their writing in all the ways listed here. To manage these various levels of revision, it is crucially important that you get an early start on your papers so that you have time to make any substantive, large-scale revisions that might be needed. Good writers also understand that revision is an ongoing process, not necessarily something that you do only after your first draft is complete. You might find, for example, that you are stuck halfway through the first draft of your paper. You decide to take a look at what you have so far. As you read, you find that you have neglected to make a point that is essential to the success of your argument. You revise what you have written, making that point clear. In the end you find that your block, your "stuckness," is gone. Why? Maybe it is gone because what was blocking you in the first place was a hole in your argument. Or maybe it is gone because you gave your brain a break. In any case, stopping to revise in the middle of the drafting process often pays off.

Developing a Critical Eye

We have yet to address the matter of how a writer knows what she should revise. Developing a critical eye is perhaps the most difficult part of the revision process. But having a critical eye makes you a better writer, reader, and thinker. So it is worth considering how you might learn to see your own work with the objectivity that is essential to successful self-criticism.

The first step in developing a critical eye is to get some distance from your work. If you have planned your writing process well, you will have left yourself a day or two to take a break before the assignment is due. If you do not have this luxury, even an hour of video games or a run over to the printing center to pick up a hard copy of your draft might be enough to clear your head. Many writers find that their mind keeps working on their papers even while their attention is turned elsewhere. When they return to their work, they bring a fresh perspective with them. They also bring a more open mind.

When you return to your paper, the first thing you will want to do is consider whether or not the paper as a whole meets your (and your instructor's) expectations. Read the paper through without stopping; don't get hung up on one troublesome paragraph. Then ask yourself the following questions:

Did I fulfill the assignment? If the instructor gave you instructions for this assignment, reread them and then ask yourself whether or not you have addressed all of the matters you are expected to address. Does your paper stray from the assignment? If it does, have you worked to make your argument relevant, or are you coming out of left field? If the instructor hasn't given you explicit instructions for this paper, you will still want to take a moment to consider what he or she expects. What books has the instructor asked you to read? What position does he or she take toward your topic? Has the instructor emphasized a certain method of scholarship (e.g., feminism, Marxism)? Has the instructor said anything to you about research methods in his or her discipline? Does your paper seem to fit into the conversation the instructor has been carrying on in class? Have you written something that other students would find relevant and interesting?

Did I say what I intended to say? This is perhaps the most difficult question you will ask yourself in the revision process. Many of us think that we have indeed said what we intended to say. When we read our papers, we are able to fill in any holes that might exist in our arguments with the information we have in our heads. The problem is that our readers sometimes don't have this same information in mind. Your challenge in revising your own writing, therefore, is to forget about what you *meant* and see only what you actually *wrote*—the meaning has to be right there in the words on the page. It is very important to think carefully about what you have said—and to think just as carefully about what you haven't said. Ask yourself the following questions: Was I clear? Do I need to define my terms? Has every stage of the argument been articulated clearly? Have I made adequate transitions between my ideas? Is my logic solid—is it there for all to see? If the answer to any of these questions is no, then you will want to revise your draft.

What are the strengths of my paper? In order to develop a critical eye you need to be able to determine when you have written well and when you have written poorly. You might find it beneficial to make a list of what you think you have done well in your draft. You might also pick out your favorite or strongest paragraph. When you find a good passage, think about why it is good. You will gain an understanding of what it means to write well; just as important, you will also be giving yourself a pat on the back—something that is very important to do in the revision process.

What are the weaknesses of my paper? Looking for weaknesses isn't as fun as looking for strengths, but it is necessary to the revision process. Again, try to make a list of what you haven't done well in this paper. Your list should be as specific as you can make it. Instead of writing "problems with paragraphs," you might say "problems with unity in my paragraphs," or, even more specific, "problems with the transitions between paragraphs 3 and 4, and 12 and 13." You should also force yourself to determine which paragraph (or sentence) you like least in the paper. Figure out why you don't like it, and work to make it better. Then go back through your paper and look for others like it.

Analyzing Your Work

If you have been considering the strengths and weaknesses of your paper, you have already begun to analyze your work. The process of analysis involves breaking down an idea or an argument into its parts and evaluating those parts on their merits. When you analyze your own paper, then, you are breaking it down into its parts and asking yourself whether or not these parts support the paper as you envision it.

The following checklist reiterates our earlier advice. Use it to analyze your whole paper, or use it to help figure out what has gone wrong with a particular part of the paper.

Consider your introduction:

If you are writing a research paper, does the introduction place your argument in an ongoing conversation?

If you're not writing a research paper, does the introduction establish context?

Does the introduction define all of your key terms?

Does the introduction draw the reader in?

Does the introduction lead the reader clearly to your thesis?

Consider your thesis:

Does the thesis say what you want it to say?

Does the thesis make a point worth considering? Does it answer the question "So what?"

Does the thesis provide the reader with some sense of the paper's structure?

Does the paper deliver what your thesis promises to deliver?

Consider your structure:

Make an outline of the paper you have just written. Does this outline reflect your intentions?

Does this outline make sense, or are there gaps in the logic—places where you have asked your readers to make leaps for which they have not been prepared?

Is each point in the outline adequately developed?

Is each point equally developed? (That is, does your paper seem balanced overall?)

Is each point relevant? Is each point interesting?

Underline the thesis sentence and all of the topic sentences. Then cut and paste them together to form a paragraph. Does this paragraph make sense?

Consider your paragraphs:

Does each paragraph have a topic sentence that clearly controls it?

Are the paragraphs internally coherent?

Are the paragraphs externally coherent? (That is, have you made adequate transitions between paragraphs? Is each paragraph clearly related to the thesis?)

Consider your argument and its logic:

Have you really presented an argument—an assertion worth making—or is your paper merely a series of observations or a summary?

Do you see any holes in your argument, or do you find it convincing?

Have you dealt fairly with the opposition, or have you neglected to mention other possible arguments for fear that they might undermine your own argument?

Have you supplied ample evidence for your arguments?

Consider your conclusion:

Does the conclusion sum up the main point of the paper?

Is the conclusion appropriate, or does it introduce a completely new idea?

Does the language resonate, or does it fall flat?

Have you inflated the language in order to pad a conclusion that is empty and ineffective?

Does the conclusion leave the reader with something to think about?

The final step you will want to take before submitting your paper is to make sure that the grammar, spelling, and punctuation are correct throughout and that you have formatted the paper appropriately. These details may seem frustratingly minor, but errors often cause readers to grow impatient with otherwise well-written essays. So be sure to take the time to carefully proofread your essay.

When you proofread, you need to slow down your reading, allowing your eye to focus on every word, every phrase, of your paper. Reading aloud is the most effective way to make yourself see and hear what you actually *wrote*, not just what you *meant*. As you read aloud, pay particular attention to those phrases or sentences you stumble on. It's a good bet that there's something awry in those phrases or sentences.

Remember, a computer spellchecker is not an editor; for example, the word "form" will be spelled correctly even if you meant "from." As you read, look for common mistakes—spelling errors, faulty subject-verb agreement, unclear pronoun antecedents, *its/it's* confusion, *their/there* confusion, and so on. If you have time, get the opinion of a second reader. Treat the proofreading stage as you would a word search or sudoku puzzle—that is, as a puzzle to be solved. No doubt, some errors are lurking in your prose—even professional writers find errors when they proofread their own work. Make it your mission to find them and root them out.

You will also want to format the paper correctly. Some instructors provide explicit directions about constructing a title page, choosing a font, setting margins, paginating, foot-noting, and so on. Be sure to follow these instructions care-fully. If the instructor does not provide directions, consult the *MLA Handbook*—the standard reference for writers in the humanities—for specific advice. Instructors appreciate papers that are not only well written but also beautifully presented. In academic writing, "beauty" equals simplicity: no needless ornamentation, no fancy fonts, and nothing to distract the reader from the sound of your writer's voice and the clarity of your thoughts.

9

Tools for Writing About American Literature

As the preceding chapters showed, you will encounter a number of different types of writing assignments in an American literature course. Fortunately, there are also a number of tools available to American literature scholars.

Using Specialized Language

Think back to the dinner party we talked about at the beginning of the book. Just as it is a good idea to familiarize yourself with the ongoing conversation before jumping in, it is also a good idea to make sure that when you start speaking, you understand the terms of this particular conversation. Virtually every industry, discipline, or activity has its own vocabulary, and literature is no different. Learning and using appropriate terminology will make your job as a scholarly writer much easier.

Start with the basics. If you are writing about a play, be

sure to refer to it as a play, not as a novel or short story. Learn to recognize common, frequently used figures of speech such as metaphor, metonymy, and simile; learn the differences between them and when to use them. You certainly don't need to learn every literary term all at once; just be sure to use the terminology correctly and precisely.

The following pages offer an extensive glossary of literary terms. For more complicated terminology, your instructor can offer additional assistance. The bottom line is that you should learn whatever terms you need in order to sound persuasive when you join the conversation at the dinner party.

A Glossary of Literary Terms

A

action. Any event or series of events depicted in a literary work; an event may be verbal as well as physical, so that saying something or telling a story within the story may be an event. See also *climax; complication; falling action; inciting incident; rising action.*

alexandrine. A line of verse in iambic hexameter, often with a caesura after the third iambic foot.

allegory. A literary work, whether in verse or prose, in which characters, action, and even aspects of setting signify (or serve as symbols for) a second, correlated order of concepts, persons, and actions. One of the most famous English-language allegories is John Bunyan's *Pilgrim's Progress*, in which a character named Christian has to make his way through obstacles such as the Slough of Despond to get to the Celestial City. Allegorical elements appear throughout American literature, particularly in the work of writers such as Nathaniel Hawthorne and Herman Melville.

alliteration. The repetition of usually initial consonant sounds through a sequence of words—for example, "While I *n*odded, *n*early *n*apping" in Edgar Allan Poe's "The Raven."

allusion. A brief, often implicit and indirect reference within a literary text to something outside the text, whether another text (e.g., the Bible, a myth, another literary work, a painting, or a piece of music) or any imaginary or historical person, place, or thing. Many of the footnotes in *The Norton Anthology of American Literature* explain allusions found in literary selections.

anapestic. Referring to a metrical form in which each foot consists of two unstressed syllables followed by a stressed one. Perhaps the most famous example of anapestic verse is "A Visit from St. Nicholas": "'Twas the <u>night</u> before <u>Christ</u>mas and <u>all</u> through the <u>house.</u>" A single foot of this type is called an *anapest*.

antagonist. A character or a nonhuman force that opposes or is in conflict with the protagonist.

antihero. A protagonist who is in one way or another the very opposite of a traditional hero. Instead of being courageous and determined, for instance, an antihero might be timid, hyper-sensitive, and indecisive to the point of paralysis. Antiheroes are especially common in modern literary works; examples might include the speaker of T. S. Eliot's "The Love Song of J. Alfred Prufrock" or the protagonist of Art Spiegelman's *Maus*.

archetype. A character, ritual, symbol, or plot pattern that recurs in the myth and literature of many cultures; examples include the scapegoat or the trickster (character type), the rite of passage (ritual), and the quest or descent into the under-world (plot pattern). The term and our contemporary under-standing of it derive from the work of psychologist Carl Jung (1875–1961), who argued that archetypes emerge from—and give us a clue to the workings of—the "collective uncon-scious," a reservoir of memories and impulses that all humans share but aren't consciously aware of.

assonance. The repetition of vowel sounds in a sequence of words with different endings—for example, in Sylvia Plath's "Ariel," "And *I* / Am the arrow, / The dew that fl*ies* / Suic*idal*, at one with the dr*ive* / Into the red / *Eye*, the cauldron of morning."

auditor. An imaginary listener within a literary work, as opposed to the reader or audience outside the work.

author. The *actual* or *real author* of a work is the historical per-son who actually wrote it and the focus of biographical criti-cism, which interprets a work by drawing on facts about the author's life and career. The *implied author*, or authorial persona, is the vision of the author's personality and outlook implied by the work as a whole. Thus when we make a claim about the author that relies solely on evidence from the work rather than from other sources, our subject is the implied author; for example, "In 'Life in the Iron Mills,' Rebecca Harding Davis heavily criticizes the working conditions of factory workers."

B

ballad. A verse narrative that is, or originally was, meant to be sung. Characterized by repetition and often by a refrain (a recurrent phrase or series of phrases), ballads were originally a folk creation, transmitted orally from person to person and age to age.

ballad stanza. A common stanza form, consisting of a quatrain that alternates four-foot and three-foot lines; lines 1 and 3 are unrhymed iambic tetrameter (four feet), and lines 2 and 4 are rhymed iambic trimester (three feet). Many of Emily Dickinson's poems use or adapt ballad stanza.

bildungsroman. Literally, "education novel" (German), a novel that depicts the intellectual, emotional, and moral development of its protagonist from childhood into adulthood; also sometimes called an *apprenticeship novel*. This type of novel tends to envision character as the product of environment, experience, nurture, and education (in the widest sense) rather than of nature, fate, and so on. Harper Lee's *To Kill a Mockingbird* is a famous example.

biography. A work of nonfiction that recounts the life of a real person. If the person depicted in a biography is also its author, then we instead use the term *autobiography*. An autobiography that focuses only on a specific aspect of, or episode in, its author's life is a *memoir*.

blank verse. The metrical verse form most like everyday human speech; blank verse consists of unrhymed lines in iambic pentameter. Much of Robert Frost's poetry is in blank verse, as is Wallace Stevens's "Sunday Morning."

C

caesura. A short pause within a line of poetry; often but not always signaled by punctuation. Note the two caesuras in this line from Poe's "The Raven": "Once upon a midnight dreary, while I pondered, weak and weary."

canon. The range of works that a consensus of scholars, teachers, and readers of a particular time and culture consider "great" or "major."

carpe diem. Literally, "seize the day" in Latin, a common theme of literary works that emphasize the brevity of life and the need to make the most of the present. Henry Wadsworth Longfellow's "A Psalm of Life" is a well-known example.

central consciousness. A character whose inner thoughts, perceptions, and feelings are revealed by a *third-person limited* narrator who does not reveal the thoughts, perceptions, or feelings of other characters.

character. An imaginary personage who acts, appears, or is referred to in a literary work. *Major* or *main characters* are those that receive most attention, *minor characters* least. *Flat characters* are relatively simple, have a few dominant traits, and tend to be predictable. Conversely, *round characters* are complex and multifaceted and act in a way that readers might not expect but accept as possible. *Static characters* do not change; *dynamic characters* do. *Stock characters* represent familiar types that recur frequently in literary works, especially of a particular genre (e.g., the "mad scientist" of horror fiction and film or the fool in Renaissance, especially Shakespearean, drama).

characterization. The presentation of a fictional personage. A term like "a good character" can, then, be ambiguous—it may mean that the personage is virtuous or that he or she is well presented regardless of his or her characteristics or moral qualities. In fiction, *direct characterization* occurs when a narrator explicitly tells us what a character is like. *Indirect characterization* occurs when a character's traits are revealed implicitly, through his or her speech, behavior, thoughts, appearance, and so on.

chorus. A group of actors in a drama who comment on and describe the action. In classical Greek theater, members of the chorus often wore masks and relied on song, dance, and recitation to make their commentary.

classical unities. As derived from Aristotle's *Poetics*, the three principles of structure that require a play to have one plot (*unity of action*) that occurs in one place (*unity of place*) and within one day (*unity of time*); also called the *dramatic unities*. Susan Glaspell's *Trifles* observes the classical unities.

climax. The third part of plot, the point at which the action stops rising and begins falling or reversing; also called *turning point* or (following Aristotle) *peripeteia*. See also *crisis*.

closet drama. See *drama*.

colloquial diction. See *diction*.

comedy. A broad category of literary, especially dramatic, works intended primarily to entertain and amuse an audience. Comedies take many different forms, but they share three basic characteristics: (1) the values that are expressed and that typically cause conflict are determined by the general opinion of society (as opposed to being universal and beyond the control of humankind, as in tragedy); (2) characters in comedies are often defined primarily in terms of their social identities and roles and tend to be *flat* or *stock characters* rather than highly individualized or *round* ones; (3) comedies conventionally end happily with an act of social reintegration and celebration such as marriage. The term *high* or *verbal comedy* may refer either to a particular type of comedy or to a sort of humor found within any literary work that employs subtlety and wit and usually represents high society. Conversely, *low* or *physical comedy* is a type of either comedy or humor that involves burlesque, horseplay, and the representation of unrefined life. See also *farce*.

coming-of-age story. See *initiation story*.

complication. In plot, an action or event that introduces a new conflict or intensifies the existing one, especially during the rising action phase of plot.

conclusion. Also called *resolution*, the fifth and last phase or part of plot, the point at which the situation that was destabilized at the beginning becomes stable once more and the conflict is resolved.

concrete poetry. Poetry in which the words on the page are arranged to look like an object; also called *shaped verse*. E. E. Cummings's "O sweet spontaneous" is an example.

conflict. A struggle between opposing forces. A conflict is external when it pits a character against something or someone outside himself or herself—another character or characters or something in nature or society. A conflict is internal when the opposing forces are two drives, impulses, or parts of a single character.

connotation. What is suggested by a word, apart from what it literally means or how it is defined in the dictionary. See also *denotation*.

controlling metaphor. See *metaphor*.

convention. In literature, a standard or traditional way of presenting or expressing something, or a traditional or characteristic feature of a particular literary genre or subgenre. Division into lines and stanzas is a convention of poetry. Conventions of the type of poem known as the epic include a plot that begins *in medias res* and frequent use of epithets and extended similes.

cosmic irony. See *irony*.

couplet. Two consecutive lines of verse linked by rhyme and meter; the meter of a *heroic couplet* is iambic pentameter.

crisis. In plot, the moment when the conflict comes to a head, often requiring the character to make a decision; sometimes the crisis is equated with the climax or *turning point,* and sometimes it is treated as a distinct moment that precedes and prepares for the climax.

criticism. See *literary criticism*.

D

dactylic. Referring to the metrical pattern in which each foot consists of a stressed syllable followed by two unstressed ones—for example, "<u>This</u> is the / <u>for</u>est prim- / <u>ev</u>al. The / <u>mur</u>- muring / <u>pines</u> and the / <u>hem</u>locks" in Longfellow's "Evange- line." A single foot of this type is called a *dactyl*.

denotation. A word's direct and literal meaning, as opposed to its connotation.

dénouement. Literally, "untying" (as of a knot) in French; a plot-related term used in three ways: (1) as a synonym for falling action, (2) as a synonym for conclusion or resolution, and (3) as the label for a phase following the conclusion in which any loose ends are tied up.

destabilizing event. See *inciting incident*.

deus ex machina. Literally, "god out of the machine" (Latin); any improbable, unprepared-for plot contrivance introduced late in a literary work to resolve the conflict. The term derives from the ancient Greek theatrical practice of using a mechanical device to lower a god or gods onto the stage to resolve the conflicts of the human characters.

dialogue. (1) Usually, words spoken by characters in a literary work, especially as opposed to words that come directly from the narrator in a work of fiction; (2) more rarely, a literary work that consists mainly or entirely of the speech of two or more characters.

diction. Choice of words. Diction is often described as either *informal* or *colloquial* if it resembles everyday speech, or as *formal* if it is instead lofty, impersonal, and dignified. Tone is determined largely through diction.

discriminated occasion. A specific, discrete moment portrayed in a fictional work, often signaled by phrases such as "At 5:05 in the morning . . . ," "It was about dusk, one evening during the supreme madness of the carnival season . . . ," or . . . "the day before Maggie fell down. . . ."

drama. A literary genre consisting of works in which action is performed and all words are spoken before an audience by an actor or actors impersonating the characters. (Drama typically lacks the narrators and narration found in fiction.) *Closet drama*, however, is a subgenre of drama that has most of these features yet is intended to be read, either silently by a single reader or out loud in a group setting. As its name suggests, *verse drama* is drama written in verse rather than prose.

dramatic irony. See *irony*.

dramatic monologue. A type or subgenre of poetry in which a speaker addresses a silent auditor or auditors in a specific situation and setting that is revealed entirely through the speaker's words; this kind of poem's primary aim is the revelation of the speaker's personality, views, and values. For example, T. S. Eliot's "The Love Song of J. Alfred Prufrock" consists of a middle-aged man's words to the unidentified person who is about to accompany him to an evening social event.

dramatic unities. See *classical unities*.

dramatis personae. Literally, "persons of the drama" (Latin); the list of characters that appears either in a play's program or at the top of the first page of the written play.

dynamic character. See *character*.

E

elegy. (1) Since the Renaissance, usually a formal lament on the death of a particular person, but focusing mainly on the speaker's efforts to come to terms with his or her grief; (2) more broadly, any lyric in sorrowful mood that takes death as its primary subject. An example is Walt Whitman's "When Lilacs Last in the Dooryard Bloom'd."

end-stopped line. A line of verse that contains or concludes a complete clause and usually ends with a punctuation mark. See also *enjambment*.

enjambment. In poetry, the technique of running over from one line to the next without stop, as in the following lines by Gwendolyn Brooks: "We real cool. We / Left school. We // Lurk late. We / Strike straight. We." The lines themselves would be described as *enjambed*.

epic. A long poem that celebrates, in a continuous narrative, the achievements of mighty heroes and heroines, usually in founding a nation or developing a culture, and uses elevated language and a grand, high style. Other epic conventions include a beginning *in medias res*, an invocation of the muse, a journey to the underworld, battle scenes, and a scene in which the hero arms himself for battle. A *mock epic* is a form of satire in which epic language and conventions are used to depict characters, actions, and settings utterly unlike those in conventional epics, usually (though not always) with the purpose of ridiculing the social milieu or types of people portrayed in the poem.

epigram. A very short, usually witty verse with a quick turn at the end.

epigraph. A quotation appearing at the beginning of a literary work or of one section of such a work; not to be confused with *epigram*.

epilogue. (1) In fiction, a short section or chapter that comes after the conclusion, tying up loose ends and often describing what happens to the characters after the resolution of the conflict; (2) in drama, a short speech, often addressed directly to the audience, delivered by a character at the end of a play.

epiphany. A sudden revelation of truth, often inspired by a seemingly simple or commonplace event.

episode. A distinct action or series of actions within a plot.

epistolary novel. See *novel*.

epitaph. An inscription on a tombstone or grave marker; not to be confused with *epigram, epigraph,* or *epithet*.

epithet. A characterizing word or phrase that precedes, follows, or substitutes for the name of a person or thing, such as *"slain civil rights leader* Martin Luther King Jr."; not to be confused with *epitaph*.

exposition. The first phase or part of plot, which sets the scene, introduces and identifies characters, and establishes the situation at the beginning of a story or play. Additional exposition is often scattered throughout the work.

extended metaphor. See *metaphor*.

external conflict. See *conflict*.

external narration or narrator. See *narrator*.

F

fable. An ancient type of short fiction, in verse or prose, illustrating a moral or satirizing human beings. The characters in a fable are often animals that talk and act like human beings. The fable is sometimes treated as a specific type of folktale and sometimes as a fictional subgenre in its own right.

fairy tale. See *tale*.

falling action. The fourth of the five phases or parts of plot, in which the conflict or conflicts move toward resolution.

fantasy. A genre of literary work featuring strange settings and characters and often involving magic or the supernatural; though closely related to horror and science fiction, fantasy is typically less concerned with the macabre or with science and technology.

farce. A literary work, especially drama, characterized by broad humor, wild antics, and often slapstick, pratfalls, or other physical humor. See also *comedy*.

fiction. Any narrative, especially in prose, about invented or imagined characters and action. Today, we tend to divide fiction into three major subgenres based on length—the short story, novella, and novel. Older, originally oral forms of short fiction include the fable, legend, parable, and tale. Fictional works may also be categorized not by their length but by their handling of particular elements such as plot and character. Science and detective fiction, for example, are subgenres that include both novels and novellas such as Ursula K. Le Guin's *The Left Hand of Darkness* and short stories such as Edgar Allan Poe's "The Murders in the Rue Morgue." See also *gothic fiction; historical fiction; nonfiction; romance.*

figurative language. Language that uses figures of speech.

figure of speech. Any word or phrase that creates a "figure" in the mind of the reader by effecting an obvious change in the usual meaning or order of words, by comparing or identifying one thing with another; also called *tropes*. *Metaphor, simile, metonymy, overstatement, oxymoron*, and *understatement* are common figures of speech.

first-person narrator. See *narrator*.

flashback. A plot-structuring device whereby a scene from the fictional past is inserted into the fictional present or is dramatized out of order.

flashforward. A plot-structuring device whereby a scene from the fictional future is inserted into the fictional present or is dramatized out of order.

flat character. See *character*.

focus. The visual component of point of view, the point from which people, events, and other details in a story are viewed; also called *focalization*. See also *voice*.

foil. A character that serves as a contrast to another.

folktale. See *tale*.

foot. The basic unit of poetic meter, consisting of any of various fixed patterns of one to three stressed and unstressed syllables. A foot may contain more than one word or just one syllable of a multisyllabic word. In scansion, breaks between feet are usually indicated with a vertical line or slash mark, as in the following example, which contains five feet: " Although | she feeds | me bread | of bit | terness" (Claude McKay, "America"). For specific examples of metrical feet, see *anapestic, dactylic, iambic, spondee*, and *trochaic*.

foreshadowing. A hint or clue about what will happen at a later moment in the plot.

formal diction. See *diction*.

frame narrative. See *narrative*.

free verse. Poetry characterized by varying line lengths, lack of traditional meter, and nonrhyming lines.

G

genre. A type or category of works sharing particular formal or textual features and conventions; especially used to refer to the largest categories for classifying literature—fiction, poetry, drama, and nonfiction. A smaller division within a genre is usually known as a *subgenre*, such as gothic fiction or epic poetry.

gothic fiction. A subgenre of fiction conventionally featuring plots that involve secrets, mystery, and the supernatural (or the seemingly supernatural) and large, gloomy, and usually antiquated (especially medieval) houses as settings. Examples include Edgar Allan Poe's "The Fall of the House of Usher."

H

haiku. A poetic form, Japanese in origin, that consists of seventeen syllables arranged in three unrhymed lines of five, seven, and five syllables, respectively.

hero/heroine. A character in a literary work, especially the leading male/female character, who is especially virtuous, usually larger than life, sometimes almost godlike. See also *antihero; protagonist; villain.*

heroic couplet. See *couplet.*

hexameter. A line of poetry with six feet. See also *alexandrine.*

high (verbal) comedy. See *comedy*.

historical fiction. A subgenre of fiction, of whatever length, in which the temporal setting, or plot time, is significantly earlier than the time in which the work was written (typically, a period before the birth of the author). Conventionally, such works describe the atmosphere and mores of the setting in vivid detail and explore the influence of historical factors on the characters and action; though focusing mainly on invented or imaginary characters and events, historical fiction sometimes includes some characters and action based on actual historical personages and events; also called the *historical novel*.

hyperbole. See *overstatement; understatement*.

I

iambic. Referring to a metrical form in which each foot consists of an unstressed syllable followed by a stressed one; this type of foot is an *iamb*. The most common poetic meter in English is *iambic pentameter*—a metrical form in which most lines consist of five iambs: " 'Twas <u>mer</u> | cy <u>brought</u> | me <u>from</u> | my <u>Pag</u> | an <u>land</u>" (Phillis Wheatley, "On Being Brought from Africa to America").

image/imagery. Broadly defined, imagery is any sensory detail or evocation in a work; more narrowly, the use of figurative language to evoke a feeling, to call to mind an idea, or to describe an object. Imagery may be described as *auditory, tactile, visual,* or *olfactory* depending on which sense it primarily appeals to—hearing, touch, vision, or smell. An *image* is a particular instance of imagery.

implied author. See *author.*

inciting incident. An action that sets a plot in motion by creating conflict; also called *destabilizing event.*

informal diction. See *diction.*

initiation story. A kind of short story in which a character—often a child or young person—first learns a significant, usually life-changing truth about the universe, society, people, or himself or herself; also called a *coming-of-age story.* Sarah Orne Jewett's "A White Heron" is a notable example.

in medias res. "In the midst of things" (Latin); refers to opening a plot in the middle of the action, and then filling in past details by means of exposition or flashback.

interior monologue. See *monologue.*

internal conflict. See *conflict.*

internal narration or narrator. See *narrator.*

intrusive narration or narrator. See *narrator.*

irony. A situation or statement characterized by a significant difference between what is expected or understood and what actually happens or is meant. *Verbal irony* occurs when a word or expression in context means something different from, and usually the opposite of, what it appears to mean; when the intended meaning is harshly critical or satiric, verbal irony becomes *sarcasm*. *Situational irony* occurs when a character holds a position or has an expectation that is reversed or fulfilled in an unexpected way. When there is instead a gap between what an audience knows and what a character believes or expects, we have *dramatic irony*; when this occurs in a tragedy, dramatic irony is sometimes called *tragic irony*. Finally, the terms *cosmic irony* and *irony of fate* are sometimes used to refer to situations in which situational irony is the result of fate, chance, the gods, or some other superhuman force or entity.

L

legend. A type of tale conventionally set in the real world and in either the present or the historical past, based on actual historical people and events, and offering an exaggerated or distorted version of the truth about those people and events. American examples might include stories featuring Davy Crockett or Johnny Appleseed or the story about George Washington chopping down the cherry tree.

limerick. A light or humorous verse form consisting of mainly anapestic lines of which the first, second, and fifth are of three feet; the third and fourth lines are of two feet; and the rhyme scheme is *aabba*.

limited narrator. See *narrator*.

limited point of view. See *point of view*.

literary criticism. The mainly interpretive (versus evaluative) work written by readers of literary texts, especially professional ones (who are thus known as *literary critics*). It is "criticism" not because it is negative or corrective but rather because those who write criticism ask probing, analytical, "critical" questions about the works they read.

litotes. A form of understatement in which one negates the contrary of what one means. Examples from common speech include "Not bad" (meaning "good") and "a novelist of no small repute" (meaning "a novelist with a big reputation"), and so on.

low (physical) comedy. See *comedy*.

lyric. Originally, a poem meant to be sung to the accompaniment of a lyre; now, any relatively short poem in which the speaker expresses his or her thoughts and feelings in the first person rather than recounting a narrative or portraying a dramatic situation.

M

magic realism. A type of fiction that involves the creation of a fictional world in which the kind of familiar, plausible action and characters one might find in more straightforwardly realist fiction coexist with utterly fantastic ones straight out of myths or dreams. This style of realism is associated especially with modern Latin American writers such as Gabriel García Márquez and Jorge Luis Borges. But the label is also sometimes applied to works by contemporary American writers such as Toni Morrison, Louise Erdrich, and Sherman Alexie.

major (main) character. See *character*.

memoir. See *biography*.

metafiction. A subgenre of works that playfully draw attention to their status as fiction in order to explore the nature of fiction and the role of authors and readers.

metaphor. Sometimes a general term for almost any figure of speech involving comparison; more commonly, a particular figure of speech in which two unlike things are compared implicitly—that is, without the use of a signal such as the word *like* or *as*—as in "Love is a rose, but you better not pick it." See also *simile*. An *extended metaphor* is a detailed and complex metaphor that stretches across a long section of a work. If such a metaphor is so extensive that it dominates or organizes an entire literary work, especially a poem, it is called a *controlling metaphor*. A *mixed metaphor* occurs when two or more usually incompatible metaphors are entangled together so as to become unclear and often unintentionally humorous, as in "Her blazing words dripped all over him."

meter. The more or less regular pattern of stressed and unstressed syllables in a line of poetry. This is determined by the kind of foot (*iambic* or *dactylic*, for example) and by the number of feet per line (e.g., five feet = *pentameter*, six feet = *hexameter*).

metonymy. A figure of speech in which the name of one thing is used to refer to another thing associated with it. When we say, "The White House has promised to veto the bill," for example, we use the White House as a metonym for the president and his or her administration. *Synecdoche* is a specific type of metonymy.

minor character. See *character*.

mock epic. See *epic*.

monologue. (1) A speech of more than a few sentences, usually in a play but also in other genres, spoken by one person and uninterrupted by the speech of anyone else; or (2) an entire work consisting of this sort of speech. In fiction, an *interior monologue* takes place entirely within the mind of a character rather than being spoken aloud. A *soliloquy* is a particular type of monologue occurring in drama, while a *dramatic monologue* is a type of poem.

moral. A rule of conduct or a maxim for living (that is, a statement about how one should live or behave) communicated in a literary work. Though fables often have morals such as "Don't count your chickens before they hatch," more modern literary works instead tend to have themes.

motif. A recurrent device, formula, or situation within a literary work.

myth. (1) Originally and narrowly, a narrative explaining how the world and humanity developed into their present form and, unlike a folktale, generally considered to be true by the people who develop it. Many, though not all, myths feature supernatural beings and have a religious significance or function within their culture of origin. Two especially common types of myth are the *creation myth*, which explains how the world, human beings, a god or gods, or good and evil came to be (e.g., the Iroquois or Navajo Creation Story), and the *explanatory myth*, which explains features of the natural landscape or natural processes or events. (2) More broadly and especially in its adjectival form (*mythic*), any narrative that obviously seeks to work like a myth in the first and more narrow sense, especially by portraying experiences or conveying truths that it implies are universally valid regardless of culture or time.

N

narration. (1) Broadly, the act of telling a story or recounting a narrative; (2) more narrowly, the portions of a narrative attributable to the narrator rather than words spoken by characters (that is, *dialogue*).

narrative. A story, whether fictional or true and in prose or verse, related by a narrator or narrators (rather than acted out on stage, as in drama). A *frame narrative* is a narrative that recounts the telling of another narrative or story that thus "frames" the inner or framed narrative. An example is Nathaniel Hawthorne's *The Scarlet Letter*, in which the narrator claims to have discovered a manuscript and an embroidered letter A in the Salem, Massachusetts, Custom House.

narrative poem/structure. A poem that tells a story.

narrator. Someone who recounts a narrative or tells a story. Although we usually instead use the term *speaker* when referring to poetry as opposed to prose fiction, *narrative poems* include at least one speaker who functions as a narrator. See also *narrative*. A narrator or narration is said to be *internal* when the narrator is a character within the work, telling the story to an equally fictional auditor or listener; internal narrators are usually first- or second-person narrators (see below). A narrator or narration is instead said to be *external* when the narrator is not a character. A *first-person narrator* is an internal narrator who consistently refers to himself or herself using the first-person pronoun *I* (or, infrequently, *we*). A *second-person narrator* consistently uses the second-person pronoun *you* (a very uncommon technique). A *third-person narrator* uses third-person pronouns such as *she, he, they, it,* and so on; third-person narrators are almost always external narrators. Third-person narrators are said to be *omniscient* (literally, "all-knowing") when they describe the inner thoughts and feelings of multiple characters; they are said to be *limited* when they relate the thoughts, feelings, and perceptions of only one character (the central consciousness). If a work encourages us to view a narrator's account of events with suspicion, the narrator (usually first-person) is called *unreliable*. An *intrusive narrator* is a third-person narrator who occasionally disrupts his or her narrative to speak directly to the reader or audience in what is sometimes called *direct address*.

nonfiction. A work or genre of prose works that describe actual, as opposed to imaginary or fictional, characters and events. Subgenres of nonfiction include biography, memoir, and the essay. See also *fiction*.

novel. A long work of fiction (approximately 40,000-plus words), typically published (or at least publishable) as a stand-alone book; although most novels are written in prose, those written as poetry are called *verse novels*. A novel (as opposed to a short story) conventionally has a complex plot and, often, at least one subplot, as well as a fully realized setting and a relatively large number of characters. One important novelistic subgenre is the *epistolary novel*—a novel composed entirely of letters written by its characters. Another is the *bildungsroman*.

novella. A work of prose fiction that falls somewhere in between a short story and a novel in terms of length, scope, and complexity. Novellas can be, and have been, published either as books in their own right or as parts of books that include other works. Henry James's *Daisy Miller* is an example.

O

octameter. A line of poetry with eight feet: "Once u- | pon a | midnight | dreary | while I | pondered | weak and | weary."

octave. Eight lines of verse linked by a pattern of end rhymes, especially the first eight lines of an Italian, or Petrarchan, sonnet. See also *sestet*.

ode. A lyric poem characterized by a serious topic and formal tone but without a prescribed formal pattern. Examples include Robert Lowell's "The Quaker Graveyard in Nantucket" and James Wright's "A Centenary Ode: Inscribed to Little Crow, Leader of the Sioux."

oeuvre. All of the works verifiably written by one author.

omniscient narrator. See *narrator*.

omniscient point of view. See *point of view*.

onomatopoeia. Word capturing or approximating the sound of what it describes; *buzz* is a good example.

overstatement. Exaggerated language; also called *hyperbole*.

oxymoron. A figure of speech that combines two apparently contradictory elements, as in *wise fool*.

P

parable. A short work of fiction that illustrates an explicit moral but that, unlike a fable, lacks fantastic or anthropomorphic characters. Especially familiar examples are the stories attributed to Jesus in the Bible—about the prodigal son, the good Samaritan, and so on.

parody. Any work that imitates or spoofs another work or genre for comic effect by exaggerating the style and changing the content of the original; parody is a subgenre of satire. Examples include *Scary Movie*, which parodies horror films, and *The Colbert Report*, which spoofs conservative talk shows. T. S. Eliot's "The Wasteland" parodies a number of contemporary genres.

pentameter. A line of poetry with five feet.

persona. The voice or figure of the author who tells and structures the story and who may or may not share the values of the actual author; also called *implied author.*

personification. A figure of speech that involves treating something nonhuman, such as an abstraction, as if it were a person by endowing it with humanlike qualities, as in "Death entered the room."

plot. The arrangement of the action. The five main parts or phases of plot are exposition, rising action, climax or turning point, falling action, and conclusion or resolution. See also *subplot*.

plot summary. A brief recounting of the principal action of a work of fiction, drama, or narrative poetry, usually in the same order in which the action is recounted in the original work rather than in chronological order.

poetry. One of the three major genres of imaginative literature, which has its origins in music and oral performance and is characterized by controlled patterns of rhythm and syntax (often using meter and rhyme); compression and compactness and an allowance for ambiguity; a particularly concentrated emphasis on the sensual, especially visual and aural, qualities and effects of words and word order; and especially vivid, often figurative language.

point of view. The perspective from which people, events, and other details in a work of fiction are viewed; also called focus, although the term *point of view* is sometimes used to include both focus and voice. The point of view is said to be *limited* when we see things only from one character's perspective; it is said to be *omniscient* or *unlimited* when we get the perspective of multiple characters.

prose. The regular form of spoken and written language, measured in sentences rather than lines, as in poetry.

protagonist. The most neutral and broadly applicable term for the main character in a work, whether male or female, heroic or not heroic. See also *antagonist; antihero; hero/ heroine*.

psychological realism. See *realism*.

Q

quatrain. A four-line unit of verse, whether an entire poem, a stanza, or a group of four lines linked by a pattern of rhyme (as in a sonnet).

R

realism. (1) Generally, the practice in literature, especially fiction and drama, of attempting to describe nature and life as they are without idealization and with attention to detail, especially the everyday life of ordinary people. See also *verisimilitude*. Just as notions of life and nature differ widely across cultures and time periods, however, so do notions of what is "realistic." Thus, there are many different kinds of realism. *Psychological realism* refers, broadly, to any literary attempt to accurately represent the workings of the human mind and, more specifically, to the practice of a particular group of late nineteenth- and early twentieth-century writers including Joseph Conrad, Henry James, James Joyce, and Virginia Woolf, who developed the stream of consciousness technique of depicting the flow of thought. See also *magic realism*. (2) More narrowly and especially when capitalized, a mid- to late nineteenth-century literary and artistic movement, mainly in the United States and Europe, that championed realism in the first, more general sense; rejected what its proponents saw as the elitism and idealism of earlier literature and art; and emphasized settings, situations, action, and (especially middle- and working-class) characters ignored or belittled in earlier literature and art. Writers associated with the movement include Gustave Flaubert and Emile Zola (in France), George Eliot and Thomas Hardy (in Britain), and William Dean Howells and Theodore Dreiser (in the United States).

resolution. See *conclusion*.

rhetoric. The art and scholarly study of effective communication, whether in writing or speech. Many literary terms, especially those for figures of speech, derive from classical and Renaissance rhetoric.

rhyme. Repetition or correspondence of the terminal sounds of words ("How now, brown cow?"). The most common type, *end rhyme*, occurs when the last words in two or more lines of a poem rhyme with each other. *Internal rhyme* occurs when a word *within* a line of poetry rhymes with another word in the same or adjacent lines, as in "The Dew drew quivering and chill" (Dickinson). An *eye rhyme* or *sight rhyme* involves words that don't actually rhyme but look like they do because of their similar spelling ("cough" and "bough"). *Off, half, near,* or *slant rhyme* is rhyme that is slightly "off" or only approximate, usually because words' final consonant sounds correspond, but not the vowels that proceed them ("phases" and "houses"). When two syllables rhyme and the last is unstressed or unaccented, they create a *feminine rhyme* ("ocean" and "motion"); *masculine rhyme* involves only a single stressed or accented syllable ("cat" and "hat"). See also *rhyme scheme*.

rhyme scheme. The pattern of *end* rhymes in a poem, often noted by small letters, such as *abab* or *abba*.

rhythm. The modulation of weak and strong (or stressed and unstressed) elements in the flow of speech. In most poetry written before the twentieth century, rhythm was often expressed in meter; in prose and in free verse, rhythm is present but in a much less predictable and regular manner.

rising action. The second of the five phases or parts of plot, in which events complicate the situation that existed at the beginning of a work, intensifying the initial conflict or introducing a new one.

romance. (1) Originally, a long medieval narrative in verse or prose written in one of the Romance languages (French, Spanish, Italian, etc.) and depicting the quests of knights and other chivalric heroes and the vicissitudes of courtly love; also known as *chivalric romance*; (2) later and more broadly, any literary work, especially a long work of prose fiction, characterized by a nonrealistic and idealizing use of the imagination;

(3) commonly today, works of prose fiction aimed at a mass, primarily female, audience and focusing on love affairs (as in Harlequin Romance).

round character. See *character*.

S

sarcasm. See *irony*.

satire. A literary work—whether fiction, poetry, or drama— that holds up human failings to ridicule and censure. Examples include Stanley Kubrick's film *Dr. Strangelove*.

scansion. The process of analyzing (and sometimes also marking) verse to determine its meter, line by line.

scene. A section or subdivision of a play or narrative that presents continuous action in one specific setting.

second-person narrator. See *narrator*.

sequence. (1) The ordering of action in a fictional plot; (2) a closely linked series or *cycle* of individual literary works, especially short stories or poems, designed to be read or performed together, as in the sonnet sequences of Edna St. Vincent Millay.

sestet. Six lines of verse linked by a pattern of rhyme, as in the last six lines of the Italian, or Petrarchan, sonnet. See also *octave*.

sestina. An elaborate verse structure written in blank verse that consists of six stanzas of six lines each followed by a three-line stanza. The final words of each line in the first stanza appear in variable order in the next five stanzas and are repeated in the middle and at the end of the three lines in the final stanza. Elizabeth Bishop's "Sestina" is an example.

set. The design, decoration, and scenery of the stage during a play; not to be confused with *setting*.

setting. The time and place of the action in a work of fiction, poetry, or drama.

The *spatial setting* is the place or places in which action unfolds; the *temporal setting* is the time. (Temporal setting is thus the same as *plot* time.) It is sometimes also helpful to distinguish between *general setting*—the general time and place in which all the action unfolds—and *particular settings*—the times and places in which individual episodes or scenes take place. The film version of *Gone with the Wind*, for example, is generally set in Civil War–era Georgia, while its opening scene takes place on the porch of Tara, Scarlett O'Hara's family home, before the war begins.

shaped verse. See *concrete poetry*.

short story. A relatively short work of prose fiction (approximately 500 to 10,000 words) that, according to Edgar Allan Poe, can be read in a single sitting of two hours or less and works to create "a single effect." Two types of short story are the *initiation story* and the *short short story* or *microfiction*.

simile. A figure of speech involving a direct, explicit comparison of one thing to another, usually using the words *like* or *as* to draw the connection, as in "My love is like a red, red rose." An *analogy* is an extended simile. See also *metaphor*.

situation. The basic circumstances depicted in a literary work, especially when the story, play, or poem begins or at a specific later moment in the action.

situational irony. See *irony*.

soliloquy. A monologue in which the character in a play is alone onstage and thinking out loud.

sonnet. A fixed verse form consisting of fourteen lines usually in iambic pentameter. An *Italian sonnet* consists of eight rhyme-linked lines (an octave) plus six rhyme-linked lines (a sestet), often with either an *abbaabba cdecde* or *abbacddc defdef* rhyme scheme. This type of sonnet is also called the *Petrarchan sonnet* in honor of the Italian poet Petrarch (1304–1374). An *English* or *Shakespearean sonnet* instead consists of three quatrains (four-line units) and a couplet and often rhymes *ababcdcd efef gg*.

speaker. (1) The person, not necessarily the author, who is the voice of a poem; (2) anyone who speaks dialogue in a work of fiction, poetry, or drama.

spondee. A metrical foot consisting of a pair of stressed syllables ("Déad sét").

stage directions. The words in the printed text of a play that inform the director, crew, actors, and readers how to stage, perform, or imagine the play. Stage directions are not spoken aloud and may appear at the beginning of a play, before any scene, or attached to a line of dialogue; they are often set in italics. The place and time of the action, the design of the set itself, and at times the characters' actions or tone of voice are given through stage directions and interpreted by the group of people who put on a performance.

stanza. A section of a poem, marked by extra line spacing before and after, that often has a single pattern of meter and/or rhyme. See also *verse paragraph*.

static character. See *character*.

stock character. See *character*.

stream of consciousness. A type of third-person narration that replicates the thought processes of a character without much or any intervention by a narrator. The term was originally coined by the nineteenth-century American psychologist William James (brother of novelist Henry James) to describe the workings of the human mind and only later adopted to describe the type of narration that seeks to replicate this process. The technique is closely associated with twentieth-century fiction writers of *psychological realism* such as Virginia Woolf, James Joyce, and William Faulkner, who were all heavily influenced by early psychologists such as William James and Sigmund Freud.

style. A distinctive manner of expression; each author's style is expressed through his or her diction, rhythm, imagery, and so on.

subgenre. See *genre.*

subplot. A secondary plot in a work of fiction or drama.

symbol. A person, place, thing, or event that figuratively represents or stands for something else. Often the thing or idea represented is more abstract and general, and the symbol is more concrete and particular. A *traditional symbol* is one that recurs frequently in (and beyond) literature and is thus immediately recognizable to those who belong to a given culture. In Western literature and culture, for example, the rose and the snake traditionally symbolize love and evil, respectively. Other symbols, such as the scarlet letter in Nathaniel Hawthorne's *The Scarlet Letter,* instead accrue their complex meanings only within a particular literary work; these are sometimes called *invented symbols.*

synecdoche. A type of metonymy in which the part is used to name or stand in for the whole, as when we refer to manual laborers as *hands* or say *wheels* to mean a car.

syntax. Word order; the way words are put together to form phrases, clauses, and sentences.

T

tale. A brief narrative with a simple plot and characters; an ancient and originally oral form of storytelling. Unlike fables, tales typically don't convey or state a simple or single moral. An especially common type of tale is the *folktale*, the conventions of which include a formulaic beginning and ending ("Once upon a time . . . ," ". . . And so they lived happily ever after."); a setting that is not highly particularized in terms of time or place; *flat* and often *stock characters*, animal or human; and fairly simple plots. Although the term *fairy tale* is often and broadly used as a synonym for *folktale*, it more narrowly and properly designates a specific type of folktale featuring fairies or other fantastic creatures such as pixies or ogres.

tetrameter. A line of poetry with four feet.

theme. (1) Broadly and commonly, a topic explored in a literary work (e.g., "the value of all life"); (2) more narrowly, the insight about a topic communicated in a work (e.g., "All living things are equally precious"). Most literary works have multiple themes, though some people reserve the term *theme* for the central or main insight and refer to others as *subthemes*. Usually a theme is implicitly communicated by the work as a whole rather than explicitly stated in it, though fables are an exception. See also *moral*.

thesis. The central debatable claim articulated, supported, and developed in an essay or other work of expository prose.

third-person narrator. See *narrator*.

time. In literature, at least four potentially quite different time frames are at issue: (1) *author time*, when the author originally created or published a literary text; (2) *narrator time*, when the narrator in a work of fiction supposedly narrated the story; (3) *plot time*, when the action depicted in the work supposedly took place (in other words, the work's temporal setting); and (4) *reader* (or *audience*) *time*, when an actual reader reads the work or an actual audience sees it performed. In some cases, author, narrator, plot, and reader time will be roughly the same—as when, for example, in 2008 we read Sherman Alexie's "Flight Patterns," a story published in 2003, set sometime after September 11, 2001, and presumably narrated not long after the action ends. But in some cases, some or all of these time frames might differ. Nathaniel Hawthorne's novel *The Scarlet Letter*, for example, was written and published in the mid-nineteenth century (1850); this is its author time. But the novel (a work of historical fiction) is set in colonial New England (1640s); this is its plot time. The novel's narrator claims to be expanding on a manuscript and an embroidered letter A that he found in the Salem, Massachusetts, Custom House during the 1840s; this is the narrator time. Were you to read the novel today, reader time would be more than 160 years later than author time and more than 360 years later than plot time.

tone. The attitude a literary work takes toward its subject, especially the way this attitude is revealed through diction.

tragedy. A work, especially of drama, in which a character (traditionally a good and noble person of high rank) is brought to a disastrous end in his or her confrontation with a superior force (fortune, the gods, human nature, universal values), but also comes to understand the meaning of his or her deeds and to accept an appropriate punishment. Often the protagonist's downfall is a direct result of a fatal flaw in his or her character.

trimeter. A line of poetry with three feet.

trochaic. Referring to a metrical form in which the basic foot is a *trochee*—a metrical foot consisting of a stressed syllable followed by an unstressed one ("Hómer").

trope. See *figure of speech*.

turning point. See *climax*.

U

understatement. Language that makes its point by self-consciously downplaying its real emphasis, as in "Final exams aren't exactly a walk in the park"; *litotes* is one form of understatement. See also *overstatement*.

unity of action. See *classical unities*.

unity of place. See *classical unities*.

unity of time. See *classical unities*.

unlimited point of view. See *point of view.*

unreliable narrator. See *narrator.*

V

verbal irony. See *irony.*

verisimilitude. From the Latin word *verisimiles* ("like the truth"); the internal truthfulness, lifelikeness, and consistency of the world created within any literary work when we judge that world on its own terms rather than in terms of its correspondence to the real world. Thus, even a work that contains utterly fantastic or supernatural characters or actions (and doesn't aim at realism) may very well achieve a high degree of verisimilitude.

verse drama. See *drama.*

verse novel. See *novel.*

verse paragraph. Although sometimes used as a synonym for stanza, this term technically designates passages of verse, often beginning with an indented line, that are unified by topic (as in a prose paragraph) rather than by rhyme or meter.

villain. A character who not only opposes the hero or heroine (and is thus an antagonist) but also is characterized as an especially evil person or "bad guy."

villanelle. A verse form consisting of nineteen lines divided into six stanzas—five tercets (three-line stanzas) and one quatrain (four-line stanza). The first and third lines of the first tercet rhyme with each other, and this rhyme is repeated through each of the next four tercets and in the last two lines of the concluding quatrain. The villanelle is also known for its repetition of select lines. An example is Elizabeth Bishop's "One Art."

voice. The verbal aspect of point of view, the acknowledged or unacknowledged source of a story's words; the speaker; the "person" telling the story and that person's particular qualities of insight, attitude, and verbal style. See also *focus*.

Additional Resources

In addition to a specialized vocabulary, scholars of American literature have a number of resources available to them. These include scholarly journals like *American Literature* and *American Literary History* and databases like the Modern Language Association International Bibliography. These resources are most likely available through your library and will help you to find secondary sources for your writing about American literature.

Another terrific resource is in the back of *The Norton Anthology of American Literature*. "Selected Bibliographies" identifies the very best reference works, histories, theory, and literary criticism on a given historical period. This section also lists some of the most important scholarship on individual authors. You should remember that these bibliographies are heavily vetted. Someone spent a lot of time thinking about which sources to include; as a result, you can assume that all of these are reliable sources. But these bibliographies also represent an infinitesimally small portion of the scholarly conversation. Think of these sources as departure points for your thinking and further research.

There are also a number of open access online archives like Making of America, HathiTrust, and Google Books, which can grant you access to primary sources. Finally, as you undoubtedly know, the Internet is a fount of endless information—and endless distraction. But, as we discussed in Chapter 4, you want to be very careful about which Internet sources you trust. For example, Wikipedia can provide some of the basic facts about a literary text; however, you shouldn't rely solely on its assessment of a text's significance, legacy, or critical history. (These assessments tend to be partial or biased or both.) As in all research, you must interrogate each Internet source carefully and thoroughly—and then cite it clearly once you write up your research.